# *The* UNFINISHED DOLLHOUSE

# *The* UNFINISHED DOLLHOUSE

## A MEMOIR OF GENDER
## AND IDENTITY

### BY MICHELLE ALFANO

*Cormorant Books*

 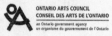

The publisher gratefully acknowledges the support of the Canada Council for the
Arts and the Ontario Arts Council for its publishing program. We acknowledge
the financial support of the Government of Canada through the Canada Book Fund
(CBF) for our publishing activities, and the Government of Ontario through the
Ontario Media Development Corporation, an agency of the Ontario Ministry of
Culture, and the Ontario Book Publishing Tax Credit Program.

LIBRARY AND ARCHIVES CANADA CATALOGUING IN PUBLICATION

Alfano, Michelle, 1959–, author
The unfinished dollhouse / Michelle Alfano.

Issued in print and electronic formats.
ISBN 978-1-77086-498-6 (softcover).— ISBN 978-1-77086-499-3 (HTML)

1. Alfano, Michelle, 1959–. 2. Alfano, Michelle, 1959- –Family.
3. Authors, Canadian (English)–21st century–Biography. 4. Parents of transgender
children–Canada–Biography. 5. Transgender children–Family relationships–
Canada.
6. Mother and child–Canada. 7. Autobiographies. I. Title.

PS8601.L37Z46 2017        C813'.6        C2016-907302-5
                                          C2016-907303-3

Cover photo and design: angeljohnguerra.com
Interior text design: Tannice Goddard, bookstopress.com
Printer: Friesens

Printed and bound in Canada.

CORMORANT BOOKS INC.
10 ST. MARY STREET, SUITE 615, TORONTO, ONTARIO, M4Y 1P9
www.cormorantbooks.com

*For River ...*

*through which all things flow*

# Contents

✤

## AUTHOR'S NOTE

*For the first third of this book, I refer to Frankie as she, although he was already self-identifying as male. As Frankie's gender identity evolves in this journey, the reader will see a notable shift in the use of personal pronouns — pre-revelation about the transition and post-revelation. Some names have been changed to protect the innocent as well as some of the guilty.*

# The Unfinished Dollhouse

✦

WHEN OUR DAUGHTER FRANKIE TURNED four, we bought her a dollhouse — the kind that you had to assemble. Her father Rob and I purchased it from a quaint shop on the tony part of Mount Pleasant Avenue in North Toronto that specialized exclusively in dollhouses and dollhouse accessories. I felt excitement in purchasing it for her. I thought she would be as enchanted with it as I am with all things small and delicate. It came in a flat, plain wooden box. It had to be built in the same manner as a real house: piece by piece. Floors, walls and partitions, windows, roof, then painting the walls, filling the house with the furniture — the beds and the tables, the tiny stove and the refrigerator, making it a home.

At Frankie's fourth birthday party, surrounded by our family, Rob and I openly disagreed about how the dollhouse should be put together and designed. Rob said we should build it, but let Frankie do whatever she liked with it in terms of painting and decoration. I was horrified by this suggestion. She was only four, I argued. She would just slap paint on it haphazardly. It would be a mess.

I saw the dollhouse as something else. I envisioned neatly painted walls of blue or periwinkle with ivory trim — like the old Victorian house I imagined we would live in one day. White framed windows on the exterior. Small, neat chairs and tables of cherry wood. A kitchen, a living room, bedrooms, all waiting to be inhabited by a family of three — mother, father, daughter, with more children to come.

Rob wanted Frankie's creativity to flow unimpeded. I wanted the dollhouse to conform to a fantasy I had about doll-houses — pretty, neat, organized, a perfect life in miniature.

Frankie displayed no interest whatsoever in the construction or design of the house. For weeks, Rob and I could not agree as to how to proceed. After three months, we just didn't. The dollhouse would never be constructed. Was that a sign that Frankie would be different from what I desired for her, from the girl I had wanted her to be? Was it also a sign that there would be no second child as I had always hoped for but could not conceive? When Frankie showed no interest in the dollhouse, I pinned my hopes on the imaginary future siblings who would, hopefully, soon come. They did not.

The dollhouse remains hidden in the closet of the middle bedroom of our Victorian house in Riverdale. Frankie never asked for it after it was first presented to her. I haven't opened up the box to see the contents since that first day at the party. Life and indifference got in the way.

# In the Valley of the Groovy Girl Dolls

✦

I HAD NO DOUBT WHEN I was pregnant that I would have a little girl. I longed for one and had done so for many years. I was superstitious enough — having experienced a miscarriage a year before Frankie was born — that I didn't have a single article of clothing or toy in the house before the birth. In my culture, that's tempting fate, spitting it in the eye and daring it to defy you. The unadorned room — cleaned, painted, and primped — and the crib were ready, but little else. I had definitely decided with Frankie there would be no pink in her wardrobe (at least none purchased by me) but still I was inundated with very pretty pale pink sleepers that I couldn't resist as gifts.

In the last trimester of the pregnancy, in the early days of November of that year, I developed pre-eclampsia, characterized by high blood pressure. This was an issue for the unborn baby. When I was sent for an ultrasound, three technicians clustered around me trying to discover the baby's heartbeat and were having difficulty finding it. In utero, she had been so small that her tiny kicks inside me felt as if the baby were flicking me with its fingers. It was a tickle rather than a robust kick. Loud sounds and music seemed to agitate her. As the technicians stood around me, talking over my prone figure and discussing this, I promptly burst into tears, fearing that they would tell me that there was no heartbeat. Finally, they jolted out of their professional demeanour and all three reassured me, as women, as mothers, that there was indeed a heartbeat but that the baby was small, so small it had been difficult to locate its heartbeat. They said the baby likely weighed less than four pounds.

The night before her birth, Rob, my sister Francesca, and I ordered and ate Greek food and I imagined what this little creature might look like when born the next day. What did I expect from my daughter as I held her for the first time in my arms? I hoped that in the future she would be smart, compassionate, kind, affectionate, loyal, family-oriented. I had expectations about how she would look too — I wanted her to be pretty, feminine, proud of her appearance. I wanted her to be all that I feared I had not been as a young girl.

I wanted to set the bar higher for her. I would never say to her if she wanted to do one thing with her life that demanded excellence and high academic standards that she should try something simpler, something more appropriate for a girl. I would never say, as a ploy to make her perform better academically if she had done very well, that she could do better. I would never imply that her life was less valuable, less noteworthy, than her brother's, should she have one. I would never say to her, "I *made* you and I can *break* you," as was said to me.

WHEN SHE WAS BORN AT three-thirty p.m. the next afternoon, Frankie was tiny, perfect, and beautiful. She was five weeks premature and weighed only three pounds, thirteen ounces. We held her exquisitely small form cupped in two hands. She was like a tiny doll in her small perfections — thin, delicate arms and legs, a halo of curly dark hair, bright, almond-shaped eyes, her skin a golden colour. I remember that when my cousin came to visit me, his youngest daughter, who was no more than four or five, was holding a doll in her hands that was bigger than Frankie.

The nurses laid Frankie down to sleep in an enclosed, incubator-like dome on a movable table beside my bed, even though she needed no assistance breathing whatsoever. The large, dome-like cover on her bed was clear and I could see her resting inside the giant bubble, a sleeping princess awaiting the kiss from a handsome prince to be awakened.

The night after she was born, the nurse gave me Demerol. I didn't know that Demerol could induce frightening hallucinations. That night I dreamt that I was on the operating table surrounded by doctors about to operate on me who wore frightening animal masks — they had faces like wolves, foxes, dogs, and other threatening animals. Unaware of what the drug could produce, I told the nurse and she took me off the Demerol the next day.

Meanwhile, Frankie's dad, who slept nearby on a comfy chair that folded out as a bed, was having more reassuring dreams. In his dream, his father came to him and told him that everything would be fine and that, despite her small size, Frankie would be fine. Frankie suffered a bit of jaundice because she was premature and was slightly sallow in colour, which gave her skin a golden hue, but she was healthy and vital in all other respects.

EVERY MOTHER BELIEVES THIS BUT I found my baby girl to be exquisite in every feature, with her little chicken-wing arms and thin drumstick legs. In the first few months of life, when lying on her side while she slept, she had this charming habit of raising her arm and her leg in tandem like a little bird as if she was ready to take flight, and then lowering both limbs again. Hence, the first of her nicknames, chicken, and sometimes, pineapple, as she was the exact size of each.

She was so tiny that she slept in a wicker basket, lined with green fabric, at the head of our bed for the first few months so that I could nurse her at night.

She needed constant nourishment to gain weight so she was breastfed every three hours, even at night. This continued for three months with one alteration — her doctor decided she was not gaining weight quickly enough and the schedule should be upped to every two and a half hours. I loved this doctor but could easily have throttled her when she suggested this as I was exhausted and emotional during the first few months. After three months, I asked Rob to take on one of the night feedings.

That was a cold, lonely winter as Rob went back to work and my mother was in another city. I didn't really know anyone in my age group who had had a baby yet so Frankie and I spent a lot of time alone. Me on the couch, reading in my little, snowbound house, and Frankie laid on a pillow beside me, sleeping. Like a princess.

I read voraciously. Frankie slept and dreamed — occasionally she would raise her arm and leg as she had in the hospital but that soon changed — her dreams of flight soon ended and she settled into her new world.

AS SHE GREW, SHE WAS funny and quirky and full of energy. She thought animals could talk and was surprised when the ducks at the Riverdale farm did not talk back to her. She was often afraid of strangers, crowds, and new situations, hugging my leg tightly and hiding her sweet little face into my thigh when a kindly stranger spoke to her. She was often the only girl invited to an all-boy birthday party, much to my mystification. Frankie loved animals but especially loved elephants in all forms — real or imagined. Did she fall in love with *Dumbo*? It was the first cartoon she saw, sitting, wide-eyed and full of wonder, with Rob and I on the couch of our little house. She loved to be hugged and kissed and I loved to hug and kiss her — she was like a beautiful doll. I could not help it — I could not believe that this exquisite creature with her golden skin and chocolate curls had come from me.

ONE INCIDENT IN FRANKIE'S YOUNG life was very telling, at least in retrospect. By six or seven, Frankie had long, beautiful, wavy dark hair that she wore in neat, carefully groomed braids, lovingly prepared by her dad each morning as she munched on her breakfast cereal or toast in front of the TV watching cartoons. She very much resembled both my sister and my mother. Frankie was particularly enamoured of the Teletubbies and would squeal with delight when she saw the baby in the sun rising up over the sky. Her hair was important to her. It had to be just so or she would fret about it all day. It was important to me too. I was proud of her beauty and that gorgeous mane of hair. She was everything that I had wished for in a daughter — pretty, playful, inquisitive, kind-hearted, and quirky; she was a great deal of fun to be around.

Once, in a very long while, she would wear her hair down and the comments she would receive were very complimentary, very positive, especially if she was wearing more traditional feminine clothing. I fancied dresses and nice shoes for special occasions for Frankie. I favoured bright colours that popped out at you, flowers and animal images on her clothes, and I loved shopping for her — special hair accessories, a new dress for the summer, colourful sandals adorned with flowers — her closet and room were a rainbow of bright colours and pretty things. I loved the too few times when she wore her hair down, even though it appeared from her reaction that it was sometimes cumbersome and uncomfortable.

One day when she was six or seven, after she had received a compliment from a stranger on the street, she told me in an absolute rage that she didn't want to wear her hair that way again. She *hated* when people said she was beautiful, she boldly declared, looking me straight in the eye. She *hated* that people noticed her. She didn't want *anyone* looking at her. This attitude mystified me. "But why," I argued with her, "if someone thinks you are pretty, would you have a problem with that? And besides," I said, in a not particularly sympathetic manner, "you *are* a pretty girl. You better get used to it."

I was not a little bemused. Angry because someone thinks she's pretty? Where was the logic in that? Would Frankie be one of those beautiful people who refused to acknowledge her beauty and its effect on those around her? Who tried to hide behind slovenly clothes, bad haircuts, and cheap eyeglasses? I hoped not. I was raised to believe in *fare la bella figura* — this literally means "to make a beautiful figure" and refers to the Italian ideal of looking good at all times, none of this hiding your light under a bushel.

Now I see that incident quite differently in light of Frankie's identification as transgender. She was unable to articulate her discomfort that day, but I think that what she was saying was that she didn't like being identified as a girl. It wasn't discomfort about *beauty*; it was discomfort about *gender*. It made her uncomfortable and the only way she could articulate that was to say she didn't want to be pretty.

She could not formulate in words the growing realization that she did not consider herself a girl and dressing her like one made her anxious, angry, furious. All I could see was the anger and that mystified me. Again, my own insecurities and needs — my own vanity and pride in her beauty — obscured what she was trying to say to me.

When I speak of this, Frankie has no recollection of the conversation at all.

FRANKIE WAS NEVER REALLY INTERESTED in dolls. She had a brief flirtation with Groovy Girl dolls but that was short-lived and eventually she gave all those dolls away — dolls, clothes, and that cute, colourful clothes closet they all happily resided in.

Groovy Girls are vaguely hippie-ish in appearance with cloth hair, bright clothing, and solid, high-heelless feet. They have more naturalistic, young girl-like curves and looks — no stilettos or lipstick for these gals. Flat-chested, multiracial, makeup-less, and age-appropriate. All the politically progressive moms in Riverdale loved them — and, conversely, had an almost fanatical disdain for Barbie.

But Barbie and I went way back. Dreamily, and fondly, I still remember a silver clutch with a pearl clasp that my own Barbie possessed in my pre-teen days. And those impossible stilettos. I liked her. She still held some fond memories for me as a pre-teen playing in the basement of our first house. It was with a delicious sense of the forbidden that I had claimed to my friend that Ken and I — as in *I, Barbie* — were getting a divorce. What a thrill a divorce was as it was strictly verboten in my large extended Catholic family.

But these professions of fondness for Barbie would only have been met with contempt or a mild pity in my circle of adult female friends.

As a girl I was completely charmed by Barbie and all her accessories. Not Frankie. As a young girl, she drew the line at the much-maligned doll. During one of her periodic toy purges — as an only child and first grandchild on Rob's side, she was completely inundated with toys of all kinds — she came across Barbies she received as birthday gifts and had never played with. She wanted them out of her closet — them and all their numerous pretty accessories.

She held up one particularly offensive blond specimen dripping in eyeliner and lipstick and declared to her father, who was assisting her in the purge, "Look at her, Daddy, she's *hideous!*" Out she went and all her little bits and pieces too — heels, purses, clothes, cellphones, jewellery — out, out, out! I had to intercede and prevent the discarding of Barbie's pink Volkswagen bug — it was too cute, I affirmed. Someone else will love this little car one day. Frankie conceded that.

But no matter, Frankie soon grew bored with the Groovy Girls and gave them away too.

Frankie wasn't particularly drawn to boys' toys either, it seemed, although we bought her trucks, Pokémon cards, Bionicles, and dinky cars, but we bought her girl stuff, too — arts and crafts sets, jewellery boxes, stuffed toys, the aforementioned Groovy Girl dolls. Here she defied the profile of many trans kids. She did not have a particular attraction to gender-specific toys. Nor did she care for toys that boys enjoyed. She had no curiosity about them whatsoever. She never asked for dolls. I wondered vaguely, but not anxiously, when she would.

When Frankie started making her own choices about clothes, she could wear whatever she liked, although I loved to see her in dresses when she was a toddler and a very young girl. That was a short but happy period — for me but not for her, it appears. At about the age of seven, Frankie started to rebel against wearing dresses. This broke my heart. Other mothers, it seemed, rejoiced in this rejection of feminine clothing by their daughters or, equally, were horrified by their young daughters donning heels, inexpensive strands of costume jewellery, and misapplied pink lipstick.

We, as parents, offered a very careful non-gender-specific environment when she was young so perhaps this was why she felt comfortable and felt no need to choose a particular path for herself. Sometimes, at the beginning, part of me still illogically believed that we set the path on which she eventually made her way by the choices we offered her. This categorically defies what trans people tell us about their own experiences — that they are who they are and parents can dress their children up or push them in a certain direction or thwart their inner desires, but the children will remain who they are inside.

# Clothes Make the Man (or Boy)

❖

ROB AND I ARE TYPICAL Riverdale parents — this is usually a
Toronto code word for the left-of-centre, middle-class, progressive people who live in our neighbourhood — not too
strenuously affirming gender-specific roles, game playing, or
clothing. We tried to excise all the "isms" that we were both
raised with — sexism, racism, heterosexism, ageism, classism —
from Frankie's life. Rob was raised in Don Mills, an aspir-
ing middle-class suburb north of Toronto, and I was raised in
Hamilton, a largely working class city southwest of Toronto.
His family has been in Canada since the First World War, mine
since the 1950s. He is a third-generation Canadian while I am
a second-generation Canadian of Italian descent. Although
our parents were, to varying degrees, conservative — they
raised us with conservative values — Rob and I were not and
we were both on the same page about how we would raise
our child. We didn't want to force Frankie into gender-specific
clothing or behaviour.

My side of the family is working class and traditional where certain codes of dress are expected for key family occasions. My female relations would not show up at a funeral in jeans. Girls and women wear dresses to weddings, bridal and baby showers, and other momentous occasions where women and girls gather to celebrate being female. I had never seen any deviations with regards to this amongst my large extended family of female relations. No one defied the unspoken code. My mother and aunts had all worked in factories or as labourers but they were always well-dressed on social occasions and family get-togethers — lipstick, heels, nicely styled hair, dresses or nice pantsuits, and jewellery.

This was a confounding dilemma for me as a mother. How to dress Frankie for important occasions? I did not understand her resistance to my requests and her frustration with my demands. What was the big deal about wearing a dress? But she loathed it and only wore them under extreme duress when we absolutely could not figure out what to wear. It would have to be very simple to meet her exacting requirements — black dress, preferably unadorned, with very flat shoes, no jewellery, no frills whatsoever. I felt as if she wanted to recede into the background as much as possible. That puzzled me.

It was a political issue for me, too. I felt Frankie was violating an unspoken rule between us about our own femininity. What was the issue with wearing dresses? I didn't feel less strong, less tough, less in control, when I wore dresses and I didn't expect her to, either. But I chalked it up to the fact that she was a tomboy and enjoyed wearing pants and shirts. I knew many women and girls who fit into this category and although I was slightly disappointed, I was not perturbed by it. In fact, my female friends always expressed enthusiastic approval of Frankie's tastes — "Hates all the girlie stuff? Great! Won't wear dresses? Even better. Despises Barbie? Terrific!" Why so? I wondered. Why are trousers better than a dress? Is a truck inherently better than a doll? Does one preference make you more fully human or more serious or more complete? Does lipstick or pearl earrings disqualify you from being taken seriously? Isn't that a sexist assumption, too?

I COME FROM A LONG line of very fierce women — most are decided matriarchs, actually — cowed by very little and very few people and most of them are quite feminine in manner and dress. They wore the pants in the family even when they didn't wear the pants. My paternal grandmother was widowed at thirty-five with five children to raise in impoverished circumstances. My mother had her own struggles, widowed at forty with three children to raise and a small, family-owned business to run. They were tough *and* traditionally feminine. When I was quite young, my mother worked in a cotton factory on the night shift, but day-to-day she dressed in a traditional, feminine manner on family outings or on special occasions when three-inch heels, pretty tailored dresses, and makeup were part of her daily routine.

No one could tell me I was being submissive or unfeminist by wearing feminine clothing and all its accoutrements. I rejected that notion categorically. Why associate power with masculine clothing? Isn't that playing into sexist stereotypes too? So Frankie's insistence on wearing pants was puzzling, although I deferred to her after a certain point. It was a bit strange and a little disturbing for me. I didn't fully understand what was happening inside that little head at the time.

I do now.

WHEN FRANKIE WAS VERY YOUNG, clad in a sweet little dress and fancy hard black shoes that I thought perfect for a wedding — Oh, how she hated those shoes! They hurt and they were constricting, I realize now — we took her to the wedding of Rob's first cousin. We were all touched by the bride's first dance with her father. She was very close to her father and they were very loving and tender with each other as they floated around the ballroom after the dinner. As we observed them from the table we had been assigned, Rob turned to Frankie and playfully asked, "How about you, Frankie, will *you* dance with Daddy like that when you get married?"

"No, never ever ever!" she replied heatedly, except the words came out "nebber, ebber, ebber" from her small mouth. Seemingly shocked at the idea, we laughed and laughed at her exclamation. How strange to think of it now, how prescient, how true.

# What Every Girl Learns

❖

AS ODD AS IT MAY seem today — picture a middle-aged, high-femme mom who wears heels and lipstick daily — I was once a somewhat rambunctious tomboy. I climbed trees. I too disdained girly clothes. I played ball on the road. I rode my battered bike along the gritty streets of my neighbourhood. I had a fort that my cousin Ana and I visited daily. It was at the top of a garage, hidden by a tree, accessed only by another tree, which we scrambled onto through an alley next to the house I grew up in.

My hometown neighbourhood was not exactly bucolic — it was in somewhat-down-on-its-heels, east-end Hamilton. The railway tracks were a mere block away. There weren't many parks nearby. We played on the street mostly — from the early morning until long into the night by the light of the streetlamps in the summers. It was the kind of neighbourhood where even the girls got into fistfights at my grade school. The girls were intimidating — tough, violent, fearing no one, not even the boys — especially not some undersized immigrant kid like me who was terrified to cross them. And I was terrified much of the time.

The game I most loved to play was war, using my plastic bucket of green army figures — bayonets at the ready, round American army helmets, laden with canteens — images of World War II soldiers in all their glory. I waged war with the neighbourhood boys daily in my tiny lawnless backyard. Perhaps it was a harbinger of things to come — my own tortuous emotional relationships with boys and men.

In my recollection of this time and this game, my thoughts sometimes drift back to the homeless man who used to haunt the downtown of our city — he was most likely a veteran who had lost his legs decades before in World War II. I only made this connection in my mind many years after I left home. Back then, he was a terrifying, ruddy-faced force of nature who haunted the streets, panhandling. His face, hands, and neck were terribly grimy as was every aspect of his clothing. He often had on a battered, dark suit jacket, sourced from who-knew-where. He moved about on a shabby wooden platform with wheels. He was ferocious; if someone extended a kindness towards him, he would snarl and snap. There was a feral quality to him. Perhaps he was shamed by his own need. I saw him often and never recall him being at peace or smiling in the slightest manner. He was still at war with himself, with those who patronized him, with his fate. He was trapped in a body that he had never wanted or asked for. How agonizing it must have been for him.

OUR NEIGHBOURHOOD WAS FAIRLY ROUGH for a kid, comprised of working class immigrant families like ours and some struggling old stock families — they didn't exactly arrive on luxury liners — who didn't like immigrants very much and were outspoken about their dislike. We ate foods that were not yet considered chic. We turned brown in the sun, not lobster pink. Our grandmothers lived with us, sometimes wore sombre black, and did not speak English when accosted by some snotty-nosed, freckled boy's insults on the street. We were considered foreign and uncool and undesirable. And vulnerable, don't forget vulnerable.

I was once ordered out of my neighbourhood friend's backyard by her strawberry blond, bouffant-coiffed mother for some unknown offence. The incident puzzles me still. Did I turn too brown in the summer sun? Was it because my hair curled and did not lie flat on my shoulders but sprung about my ears in an unruly fashion? Had I matured too quickly, too noticeably for her tastes? Was it because my friend and I had once stood on the garbage cans that lined the white wooden fence on her property and peered over the fence into the next yard? I was older than my friend — her name now forgotten — and perhaps her mother thought I was the instigator of this great crime. Did the accented voice of my parents offend — did it carry too far over the gentle waves of this woman's well-manicured lawn? Or was it the smell of the foreign food that wafted over? I never learned why I had been banished. But I still recall her icy blue stare as I slunk out of the backyard, never invited to return.

That incident, that time, felt like the beginning of the end of something. Too old perhaps to play in someone's yard now. Too swarthy perhaps to be the little girl's companion. Too mature looking perhaps to be an innocent. But I assure you I was.

I, too, absolutely loathed the way my body changed when I was eleven or twelve, just as Frankie did. I developed a bosom and voluptuous curves and elicited the kind of attention that young girls fear and hate at that age. It interfered with the small joyfulness of what my life had been. People treated me differently and I was expected to play by a different set of rules that I resented very much. I would receive catcalls from some of the local boys whenever I walked down the street by myself — beyond wolf whistles or attempts to get my attention: crude, insulting remarks that were meant to demean and humiliate. They succeeded admirably in their intent. I retain an aversion to crowds of boys and men on the street, quickly changing sides of the sidewalk if I spot a group of the same.

I learned what every girl learns — that your body is not your own. It belongs to whoever feels the need to scrutinize it, desire it, judge it, insult it, even terrorize it. Sometimes the scrutiny was accompanied by a lascivious grin or smirk, sometimes by clear disgust and revulsion. But I soon learned that my body was not solely my own. It belonged to the world.

I remember Frankie's utter horror when we travelled abroad and she and her closest friend — they were not yet fourteen — were the recipients of a number of lascivious looks, lip licking, and smirks. I was shocked when Frankie

told me, but I don't believe my sister was. She tried to counsel Frankie. "That's what some men are like," she said. "You
better toughen up and have a pretty tough look ready for
them when they do that to you." She was right. Frankie did
have to toughen up.

Another thing happened when I hit that magical age of
eleven or twelve. I was forbidden to play with boys by my
mother. I was also forbidden to play boy games. I was no
longer a girl; I was becoming a woman with all the danger
that implies — potential sexual contact and pregnancy. Or
perhaps worse in my mother's eyes: the disgrace of the same
in our small tightly knit community.

In a manner, I now sometimes wonder if Frankie's fierce
embrace of his transgender identity is an attempt to escape
this and some of the ugliness girls encounter. It's treasonous
to speculate this way. This speculation might incense some
people. They would suggest that a person is not trans because
that person is reacting to a social climate or specific situation; a trans person is trans  because he or she was born this
way. But it crossed my mind many times once Frankie came
out. How wonderful it would be to escape the daily scrutiny
and assessment of one's looks as a female. To be the subject
and not the object ... what a sense of freedom that would
engender. I cannot imagine it.

Frankie hates being scrutinized, looked at, commented
on — but very much less so in a male identity. Frankie
would tell me, in an ironic twist, that he is often stared at
in a hostile manner by the girls and women but never by the
boys or men. They — the women and girls — seemingly

can't quite figure out what he is and it is unsettling for them apparently. When I discussed Frankie's gender identity with his doctor, Dr. X, he spoke of the number of young women seeking gender reassignment as "epidemic." Why are so many women turning away from roles/lives as females? Is it because girls finally have viable options? They can transform themselves with their clothes, hair and by surgical means and drugs. They can change their names. Is it because being a female can be challenging, hard, constricting? Is Frankie rejecting not just the body he was born in but everything about being a girl and a woman?

Puberty, menses, mature development of the female body, childbirth, menopause — but also judgment, harassment, appraisal, possible violence, and the response to try and conform, or not, and face the consequences of that decision from society? If a young woman had more options, would she choose this painful course in life? I wondered then: are trans boys opting for the more liberating, albeit challenging, paths as human beings? Was it treasonous of me, as his mother, to wonder if this were true? At one point it was almost as if I was trying to convince Frankie that what he disliked was what being a girl physically entailed rather than the sense that he was truly a boy. We had long, fruitless arguments where I desperately argued against his revelation and Frankie clung to his assertion that he was a boy. I learned the truth the hard way.

# Unmasked

✦

TWO MONTHS INTO GRADE SIX, twelve little girls gathered at our Victorian house for a Halloween party. It was the last year in my daughter's grade school and many of the girls would head out to different schools: public, private, or alternative. The next year they would be in middle school. The little band would soon be broken up. It was an emotional year — perhaps more so for me. I was already feeling nostalgic for what the girls had experienced together. I felt we were on the cusp of change, momentous change, but I had no idea how profound it would be.

Our house was decorated with cobwebs and realistic-looking, small, plastic black rats on the dining room table and fireplace mantle. The Halloween lights, consisting of pumpkins and skeletons, were set up across the windows, glowing orange and white. Orange candles were lit throughout the house and an ivory-coloured skull on the mantle was lit by a tea candle within. The lights were dimmed to a haunting perfection.

The girls, delighted to be going to a Halloween party at night, decided amongst themselves that many of them would go as fairies. Each would have her own colour theme — blue, yellow, pink, black, green. They swooped in in their tutus and tiaras that night shod in ballet slippers, gripping glittering wands, some of the girls wearing lip gloss and others sparkly eye makeup. Not everyone was a fairy — one was a gypsy, one was a vampire. But *most* were fairies. My daughter, ever the maverick, came as a dead punk rocker, with torn clothes, a whitened face, and black sinister eyes. Oy. *Does she have to be dead?* I asked my husband. Apparently she did.

The girls gobbled up the chips, candy, and popcorn and gathered around the monitor in the living room to sing karaoke, sounding like pint-size versions of drunken sailors as they stumbled through the songs and slurred through the lyrics with much giggling and screeching. But they had such fun. Our neighbour, who could hear their hoots of laughter, said that she had never heard girls have such a good time.

Initially Frankie shrank back, not joining in, uneasy about singing, unsure of herself. I urged her to join the group sing-ing but she demurred. "Okay," I said. "If you don't start singing in five minutes, I will do the karaoke. Like, right now, in front of your friends."

You never saw a kid jump up so fast. She sang, all right. Frankie sang like there was no tomorrow.

At the end of the night, the brightly coloured fairies, the gypsy, and the vampire all went home, drunk on candy and soda pop and bad karaoke. I blew out the candles and turned off the lights, knowing it would all be different the following year. And it would be.

FRANKIE'S HALLOWEEN ADVENTURES REMINDED ME of the first time I went out for Halloween. When I was five and went out for Halloween trick-or-treating in our old neighbourhood, my first costume was that of a fairy princess. I wore the gorgeous bridesmaid dress I had worn at my young aunt's wedding the year before. I loved all of the attention I received, but apparently I claimed to my mother at the end of that very long and exhausting wedding day that *I will never get married again!* I had learned at an early age that being adorable is a very exhausting business. This did not, however, diminish my love for all things beautiful and sparkly — then or now.

The dress was a floor length, peacock-blue chiffon dress with a matching beaded blue bodice. There might have been a tiara involved. I'm not going to lie. It was a thrill to put on the dress as I had only worn it once for the wedding and adored it. I was greeted with many *oohs* and *ahhs* and general appreciation as I went from door to door with my younger brother. The positive attention boosted my fragile ego. Not so for my little princess Frankie in her early Halloween adventures.

Frankie's first costume, when she was two, consisted of the pointy ears of a black and white cat with a portion of a costume that slipped over her shoulders. She cried the whole time because she was uncomfortable in it. Our planned visits to the neighbouring houses on our street were cut short. The Halloween tradition we established then was that Rob would take Frankie down the street — which he loved doing — and

I would give out candy to the kids at the house, which I loved doing, and that pattern suited all of us quite well for the years that followed.

A succession of animal costumes for Frankie followed: an ingenious elephant's costume and one or two other animals. But then things got interesting because the costumes Frankie chose, or asked for, followed a particular theme: no princesses, no fairies, no tutus, no eye makeup to look pretty or glamorous. In early October, as we got ready for Halloween, if I pulled out a frilly gown from the rack of Halloween costumes at the local box store, Frankie would be looking at a wizard's wand or a sword. I was not displeased, but I was a bit surprised. The only exception would be the costume of a witch one year when she was about ten. And what a charming witch she was. A certain portion of Frankie's closet is still filled to bursting with old costumes of, respectively, a ninja, Peter Pan, Harry Potter, a scarecrow, a dead punk rocker, a zombie hockey referee, and a unicorn in a business suit. (I can't even begin to describe or explain that last one.)

Not everyone was pleased with her selection some years. The year she dressed as a ninja, she answered the door with me to give out candy and we were greeted by another similarly clad ninja, who happened to be a boy. He pinned Frankie accusingly with a beady-eyed stare and pronounced, in a loud and unpleasant way, "Girls can't be ninjas!" Frankie's face dropped.

"Why not? Sure they can!" I said cheerfully as I could. *Now take the candy and scram, brat!* I was thinking and hastily moved on to the next child in line. After the boy left, Frankie asked me forlornly if that was true. "No," I said, "it's not. You can dress as anyone you like. Forget him, he's just jealous because your costume is so great." It was, too. It helped, of course, that I liked that she had chosen this costume.

But I could see that the boy had dampened her confidence. We, as parents, had given her no restrictions on how to dress, how to act, and now she had encountered a hostile force that told her she had to change, she couldn't do what she wanted or be who she wanted to be. Sometimes, when I wrack my brain and memories as to any signs of how things might have turned out, I think of that row of costumes in Frankie's closet. Were they an sos from Frankie to us? If I concentrate I can hear the drumbeat of those messages:

I am not comfortable in this skin.
Stop putting me in those dresses.
Stop trying to make me look pretty.
I hate those fancy shoes, I just want to wear sneakers.
Listen to me, look at what I am doing.
Are you listening to me?
Are you listening ...?

It was like she was trying to remove the mask she was wearing and I kept trying to put it back on her.

# Girls Who Are Boys
## Who Like Boys to Be Girls

❖

I REMEMBER GRADE EIGHT, THE spring of 2010, as a time of great experimentation for Frankie — her "girly" period, if you will. Frankie was now thirteen. She experimented a little with makeup — no more than a dash of dramatic black eyeliner, dark nail polish — and some jewellery — mostly bangles and numerous silver rings. As I said, I was happy when she raided my jewellery box for ideas on what to wear. Her look was a bit more Goth than glamour girl. Skinny jeans, converse sneakers, tank tops, colourful bangles, glamorously blackened eyes. Occasionally she would let her long hair down or wear a beanie with her dark, luscious braids. It was a very cool look for her.

I was secretly relieved. I thought that she was becoming less of a tomboy and resembling the girls around her more. We, as parents, often say that we want our children to be individuals, to be independent, to not be sheep who follow the rest of the crowd. This is true to an extent but, really, it's a bit of a white lie. We don't want them to stick out *too* much, to be *too* different, to be so different that they are isolated, lonely, set apart from the crowd. This was my fear.

I had always, somewhat uneasily, seen Frankie's tomboy-ishness as something that likely would fade as she grew older — just as mine had. (Actually, mine had been forced out of me, but you get the gist.) What I secretly wished was that she would develop into the sort of person I personally wanted to be perceived as: strong, tough, but feminine in appearance. So these slight changes in her demeanour seemed to be a move in that direction.

She, also, for the first time, expressed an interest in boys — in one boy, specifically. And oh, what a boy. I could see the heartache coming from a mile away. Let's call him Quinn.

Quinn was very good looking — in the young Justin Bieber mode: thick, carefully groomed hair, very nice clothes, angelic looks, great smile. Many, many girls in Frankie's circle were enamoured of him. But he had a nasty track record: he had broken the hearts of several of Frankie's friends. And in quick succession. A couple of months here, a couple of months there, and poof! He was on to the next one after the emotional devastation. Frankie and I talked about this. I warned her that as he hadn't treated her friends very well, he wasn't likely to be that nice to her either. She was nonplussed and unim-pressed by my advice — what teenager isn't, of course? I, too, at that age, had had my head turned by a pretty face, a smooth-talking boy, the promise of love and affection from a popular boy. Young girls are susceptible to this.

ROB WAS COMPLETELY AGAINST FRANKIE dating. He thought she was too young and he didn't trust Quinn. He was right on the money on both counts. But I know how sneaky teenagers can be, having been one myself, and I had a feeling that if we actively opposed this relationship it would drive Frankie's behaviour underground. I would rather they were both at our house, and within our sight, than somewhere else we didn't know about, doing something we weren't comfortable with. So we tolerated the relationship.

Then came the inevitable breakup. It was harsh and insensitive and typical of an immature male teenager in the digital age. It was the start of a long and very difficult period for Frankie. She sank into a depression. This funny, quirky, interesting kid slipped deeper into a morass of inactivity, self-doubt, and anxiety. She started missing school — two or three days a week. She slowly dropped out of her extracurricular activities — including hockey, which she loved. She lost interest in her music, in playing guitar, making art and jewellery. She was reluctant to attend family get-togethers and social activities. She stopped seeing friends, close or otherwise.

She complained of many ailments — exhaustion, stomach aches, headaches, insomnia, interrupted sleep. Her foot hurt, her head hurt, her chest hurt. We had her examined, had blood tests done for anemia and iron deficiency and examinations for possible muscular strain in her foot. Numerous times. We even had her wear a heart monitor over two or three days to try and determine the source of her chest pain.

Nothing. Nothing. Nothing. It was maddening and frightening. What was happening to her? I couldn't even formulate the word in my mind, I refused to go there. But I knew the truth. My child was depressed. I was struggling in my own mind with even acknowledging it. Her eyes were dull and expressionless. Her energy level was diminished. Her skin was pale and sallow. She lost interest in everything she loved.

She often couldn't get up for school, and even when she did manage to drag herself there, inevitably some well-meaning idiot would comment that she didn't *seem* very sick and how would she ever catch up on everything she missed? This terrified and further depressed her so that she grew afraid to go back to school. She feared the teachers thought she was malingering. She seemed unable to articulate what was wrong with her to us or anyone.

We had two different responses towards her state: initially, the gentle, cajoling response trying to ease her out of bed each morning. This was usually me. Then we tried the tough-love approach. This was usually Rob. Neither method worked very well. We went up and down the stairs five, six, seven times each morning trying to get her up and out of bed only to be met with a defeated, exhausted, weeping child who could not rouse herself. We would start at seven-thirty a.m. and work on getting her up steadily until nine a.m. and then give up and shamefacedly call the school to report her absence.

We both began to loathe and fear the phone call to the school that had to be made each morning. It became a battle as to who would make the call. We fought about it. *It's your turn. No, it's your turn,* we snapped at each other. We both dreaded making that call, even though they were nothing but neutral in tone and accommodating. I was afraid they were judging me. *What's wrong with your kid?* I imagined they were thinking. It was like an admission on our part that we had no control and could have no effect on her behaviour. It rankled.

If anyone tried to give me advice about getting Frankie out of bed I found myself perilously close to punching them in the nose. Have you ever tried to get a teenager out of bed if she didn't want to be up? Give it a try sometime and let me know how it goes. The two biggest child experts in the world are the childless and those parents who don't have to deal with the issue you have with your own child.

Frazzled and frightened, Rob and I began to turn on each other.

"You're too soft on her. She starts crying and you immediately give in."

"You have no idea how she's suffering, you've never experienced depression like this."

"She will fail this grade and it's our fault for not being tougher on her."

"You're insensitive and mean."

At one point Rob turned to me and said, "I see now why people with a sick kid end up splitting up."

It was not a threat, just a painful, unhappy observation with the ring of truth.

Finally, the sympathetic vice-principal at Frankie's middle school recommended a counsellor at Delisle Youth Services who specialized in teenagers and their emotional health issues. Frankie started seeing the counsellor in the early summer of

2010, after I practically begged the counsellor to move us up the waiting list. At last, there was some relief after months of anxiety.

ONE OR TWO INCIDENTS STAND out from the spring and summer when Frankie was getting counselling from Delisle. On Easter Sunday, Frankie had had a full-blown meltdown in the car. We were to spend the day at my mother's home, as was our tradition as a family. I had made food — as had both of my siblings and mother — for a potluck dinner to be held at my mother's condo outside of Toronto. I had bought Easter chocolates for Frankie, her two cousins, and my sister, as well as a pot of beautiful Easter lilies for Mom.

It was clear from the moment she reluctantly got up that morning that Frankie did not want to go out. Not because she didn't want to see my family — she just didn't want to leave the house. We had been experiencing this behaviour since her breakup with Quinn in February. She lost interest in everything except her computer. She pleaded to be left behind, but I very much wanted her to come to my mother's. She was spending far too much time alone in her room and it was worrying me. When we got in the car, Frankie started to get very anxious and began to cry. When we were on the road she begged us to turn the car around and go home. It began as quiet pleading, followed by more crying, which eventually escalated into full-blown weeping and distraught screaming. By this time, we were halfway there. I said, "No, we are not turning the car around." I dug in my heels. So did Frankie.

She started to buck and writhe like a toddler in a car seat having a tantrum. I had never seen this behaviour before outside of her toddler years. She was screaming that her foot hurt. *Again with that damn foot*, I thought. Truly frightened, I climbed into the back, with Rob driving the car down the highway at ninety kilometres an hour, to try and calm Frankie, but she refused to be consoled or persuaded. She kept begging us to turn the car around. Then we were caught in a long, maddeningly slow, traffic snarl curling its way westward on the Queen Elizabeth Way. We soldiered on.

It was a harrowing ride. Frankie refused to leave the car when we arrived at our destination. I said, "Look, just let me drop off the food and gifts and then we can leave. You stay here with Daddy." She quietly obliged. Convinced that we would not force her, she stopped crying and finally calmed down. I hurried upstairs with my arms full, but by the time my astonished family opened the door I had burst into tears and had no coherent explanation for why we couldn't join them for dinner. They were shocked and upset at my appearance and completely confused. While I was trying to formulate some credible story — all I could muster was that Frankie was not well and we had to go home — my mother snuck downstairs to the car and was gently urging Frankie to come upstairs just for a quick bite. Frankie quietly refused and would not say what was wrong.

Upstairs with me, my extended family was stricken, speechless. They had no idea what was transpiring in our home and could make no sense of my explanation. My sister knew some of what was happening but kept mum. They were upset and confused — as was I. I had never experienced this level of anxiety in Frankie. My mother, who had returned upstairs to her apartment, finally released me by casually joking that mothers of only children were *so* sensitive about their children's illnesses. I knew she was trying to shield me from further questions and I was immensely grateful. We returned home with no further drama.

# Taking Down Peter Rabbit

✦

AROUND THE TIME THAT FRANKIE fell ill, she started to purge things in her room that she felt were too childish for her. My old friend Peter Rabbit, who had adorned the light switch plate in front of Frankie's room since her birth, would have to come down soon, I surmised in light of the purge. I was surprised that Frankie had not insisted yet. I think it had escaped her notice. Every once in a while I would see it and think, *I really should do that — take it down, put up something more age-appropriate for Frankie.* What that would have been eluded me.

At one point Frankie went through her room and started removing things I had placed there over the years: a few golden cupids that I hand painted for her, a framed drawing of the Madonna with child given to me by a friend, a drawing of Victorian-era angels, certain books and games she now found childish. Apparently, she missed Peter Rabbit in her sweep of the room. It was inevitable, of course, but I had to admit it smarted a bit as she sheepishly handed me the pile of things she preferred to not have in her room. I could see she felt a little guilty. Maybe it was my crestfallen look that I wasn't able to erase quickly enough.

I remember how much pleasure it gave me to decorate her room with stuffies and clean, white bed linen for her crib. Pillows and toys, new books and games. Special hangers for her little clothes. A trio of heart-shaped boxes. The cupids and drawings. Paintings and pretty pictures.

My child was now into Guitar Hero and dance music. She had the Jonas Brothers and hip hop on her iPod. She surfed YouTube for funny videos and posted on Facebook. She was on MSN Messenger and for a time wrote on her own blog about books she liked that dealt with tweenie problems and issues. She was definitely not into Beatrix Potter or cute bunnies.

It seemed too selfish to cling to this little figure when she probably didn't want it there. But I was glad she had not mentioned it right away. I wanted to hang on to him a bit longer. *Maybe she wouldn't notice for a while*, I thought.

AROUND THIS TIME, FRANKIE EMBRACED vegetarianism. I wouldn't say the concept was foreign to me; some of my relations and friends are also vegetarians. But I feel a little like the aunt in *My Big Fat Greek Wedding* on learning that the groom did not eat meat. "Okay," she says agreeably, "No problem, I cook lamb!" I am a bit mystified by the religious fervour that seizes vegetarians. Rob and I weren't vegetarians and, to be honest, I have a somewhat low tolerance for vegetarian demands in my kitchen.

I was a bit stymied on how to address Frankie's very real

moral concerns, even though I did not agree with them. Luckily, her father is more tolerant and resourceful than I am and together we prepared meat-free, protein-rich meals to satisfy her requirements — substituting beans, tofu, eggs, peanut butter, cheese, and fish for meat. No small task. Rob and I decided that we would get our carnivore fix outside the home, away from Frankie so that she wouldn't be disturbed by it.

However, I had surmised that either because of the stress that Frankie was under — the breakup with Quinn, the onset of the depressive episodes — or the hormonal stresses of being a teenager, she wasn't faring well on this particular diet. One day, when I was combing her hair and putting it in braids, I noticed a quarter-sized bald patch where her hair parted in the middle of her head. I didn't say anything to Frankie but mentioned it to her dad and asked him to look at it discreetly. He did. He saw it too. Eventually I raised it with Frankie and I said we should address it with the doctor.

There was another disturbing element that may or may not have been related — Frankie's periods, never delightful at the best of times, became much more painful, debilitating, and difficult to manage. Over several weeks, as things did not remedy themselves I went to see the nurse at Frankie's doctor's office. She usually handled queries of a non-urgent nature such as these. We saw her more often than we saw the doctor, whom we liked very much. The doctor was a gentle person who had delivered Frankie and was exceptionally kind to her. Competent and knowledgeable, I usually also got very good advice from the nurse, but on this day she seemed in a particularly testy mood. When I came to see the nurse, I had a mental list of things to check with her.

The nurse did a cursory examination. She was clearly in a bad mood that day and this did not bode well. Perhaps her workload was excessive, but she had become increasingly unfriendly and was starting to treat my cautious inquiries as though they were idiotic inconveniences posed by an overly neurotic mother. At least that's how she made me feel.

"Is it the new diet?" I volunteered timidly. I was starting to feel foolish for bringing Frankie in. "Frankie's become a vegetarian."

"No," she answered testily.

"But I was reading ..."

"There is no connection between that and the hair loss."

"Is it stress? She's been very stressed lately."

"Maybe. Could be," she said indifferently.

"Is it the way she combs her hair? The parting of her hair in the same spot is perhaps aggravating her scalp, her hair line?" At this time Frankie had been wearing her hair in two long braids with a severe part down the middle for six or seven years. My stylist had suggested that the continued pressure on the same points of her hair and head might have led to this hair loss. She had seen it before with similar styles. Here the nurse looked at me like I was an idiot.

"Is there *anything* we can do?" I asked somewhat desperately.

"No," she said flatly and offered me absolutely no guidance to alleviate the situation.

I left the office deflated and confused. Chock up another public relations victory for the medical community, I thought

sourly. So we muddled along and did what we thought best —
we took Frankie off the vegetarian diet. We altered her hairstyle
slightly to change the part. We found a cream that allegedly
stimulated hair growth and we put beef and other meats back
on the menu, much to Frankie's chagrin. Eventually her hair
grew back, but very slowly.

And as I believe in voting with my feet when I am dissatisfied with the treatment I receive at the hands of medical
professionals, I switched doctors.

Several years later, I learned that the hair loss Frankie
experienced was because she had been pulling her hair out
due to the stress she was under. She had been too afraid to
tell me.

# Summertime Sadness

❖

AS GRADE EIGHT GRADUATION IN the summer of 2010 approached, Frankie seemed somewhat better. Was it the prospect of middle school finally ending? Not seeing Quinn anymore as he was going to a different local high school? Was it our trip to Italy that she was anticipating in June and July with family and friends?

At her graduation ceremony in June, Frankie truly looked beautiful — wearing a simple off-white dress that came to the knee and ballet flats. She wore her long, dark hair down, her skin was glowing, and her perfect, white teeth were flashing. We took a series of photos of her that day: Frankie with her two best friends; Frankie with her dad and the two girls' fathers; and Frankie with the girls' mothers and me. Examining those photos you would have no idea she had been ill and missed most of the spring session at school. Looking closely at the photo now, I appear to have an iron grip on Frankie's arm and an odd expression on my face while she smiles at the camera beatifically.

In the summer, the youth counselling seemed to help some-what, although Frankie remained subdued in her interactions. Teresa, her counsellor at Delisle, was a lovely, sympathetic young woman with a gentle manner. We had an initial meeting in a generically cheerful office with encouraging posters espousing positive attitudes towards life lining its hallways. Frankie would meet her separately in hour-long sessions, while one of us waited in the reception area or in the public library on the ground floor. After a time, I asked Teresa if she had any idea what had been troubling Frankie. She said that she did but that their conversations were confidential and Frankie specifically had asked that she not speak of it to us. We were stuck. There *was* a source to her anxiety, but Frankie was uneasy speaking about it to us and we couldn't pursue it with her without causing some distress.

After our trip to Italy in June and July, the summer was mostly uneventful and we decided to let Frankie have a peace-ful, less anxious summer. No schedule, no extracurricular activities, lots of sleep and rest, lots of time spent with friends she missed. It was low-key, quiet, and relatively calm. She seemed truly excited to be going to her new high school — an arts-oriented school just a twenty-minute TTC ride from home. The school was set in an upscale neighbourhood in the east end of Toronto on beautiful grounds and offered a number of artistic disciplines for kids interested in the arts: music, drama, dance, visual arts, singing. The students had a reputation for being interesting, artistic. The open house the school held impressed us both — the kids who performed that night for the parents and prospective students were talented and engaged and the principal impressed me with his enthusiasm and general *bonhomie*. It seemed a good fit for Frankie and her interests.

But, for some reason, a chill ran through me the first week of school when Frankie announced that she was happy. She liked her school, she liked her teachers, she liked her arts-oriented classes — she chose to play the violin — and the courses she had selected in the visual arts. This would be a pattern I would see several times in the course of the next few years: joy, contentment, and then a plunge into something darker and more disturbing.

FRANKIE'S ILLNESS BROUGHT ME BACK to the first few weeks of her life, when her health was precarious. When she was born, I could hold her in one hand because she was that tiny; she weighed less than four pounds. I knew that whatever affected her would affect me profoundly, both physically and emotionally, for the rest of my life. She was a preemie and undersized, born five weeks early. She was the exact size of a chicken — hence her nickname and woe to me if I ever tried to call any other child that name affectionately. The doctor had decreed that once we were released from the hospital she had to come back every day to have her blood tested for the bilirubin level because of her jaundice, as elevated levels could indicate certain diseases or ill health. This was not unusual for a preemie; stressful, but not unusual.

The nurse who was required to take her blood sample would grasp Frankie by the heel — some might say professionally, I would say roughly and coldly, how I loathed that woman for the way she handled her — and plunge the syringe into the meat of her tiny heel, withdrawing the blood that had to be tested. Frankie, of course, wailed and I would start crying and Frankie's poor father had two females to console as we both held her in our arms. It was the first time I had felt someone else's pain so keenly.

This went on for weeks until the jaundice receded — poor little mite, born just before winter started in a very cold year. If she had had more exposure to sun she might have healed more quickly. As it was, I was afraid to take her out into the cold weather; she was so small and it was so cold. I had no friends with children that age. It was a lonely winter — just Frankie and me in the little house in Riverdale surrounded by a small mountain of snow and ice.

If she cried, I carried her in one hand, cupping her head in the other hand and whispering endearments into her ear; this seemed to calm her. I would carry her around on a pillow, like a wee princess, and rest her on the sofa in a shaft of sunlight beside me as I read. I read a great deal that winter. Her little diapers drooped — she was too tiny and they didn't manufacture anything that small. Her clothes were ill-fitting. She looked like a doll that had been placed in clothes too large for her tiny frame.

One day I showed Frankie her first bed: a large straw basket swathed in green cloth. It resembled the basket of reeds that Moses was found in in *The Ten Commandments* and it had sat at the headboard of our bed every night during the first few months of her life. When I showed it to her, she couldn't believe she had slept in it. By then she was as tall as me and was absolutely delighted when people said that maybe she would be as tall as her father one day.

Not much had changed, in a way; I couldn't bear to look at a cut on her skin or think of her in pain of any kind. Her suffering was unbearable to me. That anyone should hurt her infuriated me and summoned up a dark and implacable desire for revenge. When she was ill with strep throat, I found it hard to contain my anxiety. Familial illness provokes this in me. My mother was not well either at the time and was finding it difficult to stand without the use of a walker. Both of my "girls" were likely to be okay, but still there was that nagging worry. What if it was something else, what if it was more serious and we just didn't see it? The illness seemed interminable. Frankie looked so weary, so fatigued with resisting it.

Filmmaker David Cronenberg was once queried about the obsession with illness and disease that seems to pervade his films. The interviewer asked him if he often thought of disease and the possible death of his family members and he responded, "Every day." I understand that sentiment now. I understand that undercurrent of anxiety and the desire to take away a family member's pain and carry it for them.

# Juliet Squared

✦

GRADE NINE TURNED OUT TO be a challenging year, despite Frankie's initial optimism and pleasure at being at the arts high school. A few weeks into the school year, Frankie began to falter — missing classes, exhibiting social anxiety about attending school, having low self-confidence about completing assignments and meeting new people. Where had all the optimism regarding the new school disappeared to? It was gone — like a teenager's first puff on a cigarette.

I turned to the vice-principal of Frankie's school for guidance on how to proceed. Frankie could not complete the year if we didn't do something quickly. The vice-principal, who was firm and no-nonsense but not unsympathetic, recommended that Frankie speak to the guidance counsellor — an affable woman with the tight fussy curls of an older lady's smalltown coiffure, a pleasant manner, and an east coast accent. I liked her very much — she seemed cheerful and engaged with a genuine interest in the students.

There we met the same impediment as we had with the

youth counsellor during the previous summer. After two or three sessions, Frankie had confided in the counsellor, who said she could not break Frankie's confidence by telling us what Frankie's issues were; however, she told me jovially over the telephone, "When you find out, you'll just find the whole thing funny."

Rob and I were mystified by this bold assertion. Frankie was so distraught and miserable that she failed to complete assignments or attend classes, missed her hockey games, and avoided family gatherings. When we found out, the counsellor assured us, we'd find the thing that was distressing her funny? But Frankie had not told the counsellor the whole truth — it was a partial truth, and that partial truth, it appears, was not something that overly concerned the counsellor.

When I think back, I believe the situation was that we — my small family of three — lived in a lovely, liberal bubble in a pocket of relatively strife-free, middle-class Toronto. I cite Frankie's school in particular, which is refreshingly free of bullies and bigots and has a zero tolerance policy for anything of that sort. Like rich people who prefer to hang out with rich people, liberals and progressives prefer to do the same. In our own somewhat narrow-minded way, to live otherwise would be intolerable. Frankie's revelation was no large concern for this woman, was almost laughable to her, whom I imagine had seen much worse ills amongst the students. At least, that is what I told myself in more charitable moments, which were few and far between, when I thought of her.

WE THOUGHT WE HAD FOUND an ally in the guidance counsellor, but when Frankie would show up at her door and ask
to sit for a while rather than go to classes, she was told to
push herself to go to class and that when she did so she would
feel better. This was another tough-love approach that failed
miserably. We all felt she was not taking Frankie's concerns
seriously. Instead of going to class, Frankie remained at home
or fled school early, often pleading with me to call the school
and get her excused. There were teary rides to school in the
morning with Frankie literally pleading with us to return
home. More often than not, if we roused her to get to school
we would end up driving back home and depositing her in
her bed.

This created an extra stressor for Rob, who worked at home
at the time. He faced the spectre of this unhappy, depressed
teenager who could not be roused until noon, ate little, and
interacted with very few people. Aside from his worry, there
was the added oppression of feeling he could do nothing to
help her. At least I was able to leave the house, go to work,
and focus on other issues. For him, it was impossible to forget
that our child was not well. Frankie had ended her counselling sessions at school, insisting she didn't need them and they
were a waste of time.

DESPITE THE SCHOOL GUIDANCE COUNSELLOR'S assertion, none
of Frankie's physical ailments were receding — pains in her
chest, the mysterious pain in her foot, stomach aches, headaches. There was still the emotional element: weepiness,
irritability, depressive moods, social anxiety. Months into the

school year, struggling as we all were, Rob came to me with a disturbing revelation.

Frankie had been using her dad's computer and had left a screen open with a message to an unknown girl, identified only by three initials on screen. We did not recognize the initials, which was odd because we thought we knew all of Frankie's friends. The message was enigmatic but the gist of it appeared to be that Frankie had mailed the girl a gold bracelet that Frankie said she'd received from her grandmother, my own mother. The girl's mother had found the bracelet and thrown it out in a rage. This had provoked a terrible fight between the unknown mother and daughter.

These things perturbed me terribly. Who was this mystery girl and why had Frankie given away a gift from my mother? Why was the mother so provoked? What were we to do here? Rob didn't feel comfortable asking Frankie about what he had seen on his computer. Frankie had been particularly adamant about her privacy of late and having a private space where she could be on her computer without having a parent peering over her shoulder. We felt that this was a fair request.

But Rob felt there was something in the message that suggested intimacy, which suggested that Frankie had an intimate relationship with this girl. We said nothing to her. We didn't know, we only suspected the nature of their relationship. I can't say we were shocked, though we were, perhaps, surprised — yes, surprised. But then Frankie's behaviour became more erratic, more troubled in the following weeks. She was weepy and jittery, unable to focus, deeply unhappy. Finally, during one particularly trying episode, I pointedly asked Frankie if she was gay. She broke down completely, weeping, and said yes, yes she was.

Our suspicions were confirmed. How to describe how we felt without sounding homophobic? It's a very rare situation where a parent does not experience *some* anxiety when they learn that their child is gay or bisexual or transgender. It's more involved than simple homophobia, even though there is often an element of that — it's fear of the unknown, fear of difference, fear of isolation and prejudice and possible violence exerted towards your child who could no more alter their sexual identity than they could permanently alter the colour of their eyes. I have seen parents — who knew from the time their child was four or five that they were gay — fall to pieces when the child actually said the words, "I am gay."

But this revelation was a relief, in a way. So that was the source of her anguish, her suffering, her fear.

THERE WAS ALSO THE UNHAPPY matter of Frankie giving a gift from her grandmother to a stranger. No, no, Frankie insisted when we questioned her about the missing bracelet. That was not her grandmother's gold bracelet that Frankie had sent this girl. It was something small and inexpensive. Then the big reveal. For the last two years Frankie had been corresponding online with a girl named Julia, someone she had met at summer camp years before. Julia lived out of town and was a year younger. They were now girlfriends. Questions lingered. What had happened with the bracelet? Why was Julia's mother so furious? The mother had found the girls' online correspondence and then found the bracelet

Frankie had mailed to Julia. She was furious at the thought that Julia was gay and had tried to contact Frankie online, terrifying both girls who were, respectively, fifteen (Frankie) and fourteen (Julia).

Frankie told me that Julia's mother had begun to make bizarre demands and threats. She tried to friend Frankie on Facebook. We looked her up: the pics she offered on social media were a bit risqué and made us uneasy. The mother insisted to Frankie that she knew many police officers and was going to report her. She demanded that Frankie give her my telephone number so she could speak to me. What exactly would she say to the police, or me, for that matter? "My teenage daughter is involved with another teenage girl who plays the violin and still sleeps with her stuffies?"

I said that the mother could contact me by email but that wasn't good enough for her. She was insistent. I put my foot down. No contact with either Julia or the mother, for the time being, until things calmed down and we figured out what was happening. I blocked the mother on Facebook in case she tried to reach me that way. I was relieved we had an unlisted number. I asked Frankie not to respond to the mother in any manner and to let Julia know that they needed to take a break for a while.

Both girls went into an emotional tailspin. Julia, I learned through Frankie, who was not receiving emotional support at home, fell ill, and withdrew from family and school. Her parents refused to get her counselling, saying it was unneeded. Frankie, because she was frantic over Julia's fate, suffered terribly as well — she could not focus, she could not function normally. She felt guilty and terrified that she was the cause of Julia's problems with her mother. What a tangled mess we faced that winter — both Frankie and the unknown Julia emotional and distraught, their health in jeopardy. Some vengeful, homophobic mother out on the horizon plotting, I feared, her revenge. I felt frightened and confused by this unknown threat — trying to wrap my head around this new information. The Montagues and the Capulets didn't have anything on us.

These new and sometimes alarming thoughts kept revolving in my head: Frankie was gay. Frankie had a girlfriend. Her girlfriend's mother, and possibly father, opposed the relationship and who knew what they would do. The mother appeared homophobic, volatile, and capable of untold emotional damage to both girls.

Frankie's story of how she met Julia did not hold together for me. Frankie had often spoken of the girls she had connected with at Camp Wanakita, a summer camp, an experience she had loved, and I remembered no mention of a Julia. Frankie said that Julia was a friend of a school friend who, coincidentally, had attended the same summer camp. She had happily re-encountered her at a park near our house where a lot of Riverdale teenagers hung out when Julia was visiting friends from out of town. *Hmm, that was a strange coincidence*, I thought.

And Julia was on her own now, seemingly without a friend or protector. I felt anxious and nervous that I could not intercede for a young girl I had never met and had no real knowledge of.

# Let the Light In

✦

ON THE DAYS THAT FRANKIE could not rise from her bed, I would enter her bedroom quietly and ask her how her night had been. I would walk over, pull the curtains back to let light into the room, and try to quietly talk to her. Sometimes I sat on her bed and stroked her hair and tried to gently rouse her. I usually got little or no response. The room in the morning was always dark with an air of Juliet's tomb, I sometimes thought morbidly. It was intensely quiet — no ticking clock, no clock radio, no music, and, most importantly, no light peering in. Frankie could not sleep unless it was completely dark in her room. She struggled to rise each morning, so an alarm was futile.

I could tell from her voice what sort of day we were going to have. On bad nights, which were most nights, she would wrap herself tight in her red sleeping bag and lie on top of her bed, imbedded in a cocoon. But instead of a butterfly rising from it, an exhausted, weeping child would often do so. I tried to dissuade her from using the sleeping bag. For some reason it disturbed me — the sleeping bag was a warning flag of some sort, signalling that she was not right, that she was not comfortable in her own bed. But she refused to give it up, and grew agitated if I tried to take it away, saying she couldn't understand my insisting on its removal. Eventually I chose to ignore it. That seemed the best thing to do. Her dependence on the sleeping bag frightened me for some reason. It seemed strange and indicative of some sort of instability. It might seem an innocuous accessory, but she became highly agitated if I tried to remove it.

If she was hesitant, slow to respond to my queries, unsure, evasive in her answers, I knew that she would not be getting up that day. She would often protest that she would *definitely* go in for second period or *probably* go after lunch or *most likely* go for that crucial last period when an assignment was due but it would almost always come to nothing.

Sometimes I would argue with her a little or try and cajole her or subtly pressure her a bit — anything to get her to rise, to get a response from her. Sometimes I would leave her room, seething because I was totally ineffectual, swearing under my breath in frustration. I was caught once or twice doing so. When I was unsuccessful, which was probably three out of five school days, I would start to close the curtains again before I left the room. My reasoning was she might be able to sleep, to rest, for the morning with the hope that she would rise later, go to school, and feel better about herself.

But one day she cried out in alarm, "Please don't close the curtains!" as I was drawing them closed.

"But why?" I turned to her, alarmed by her anguished tone.

"It's like you're giving up on me," she cried. "Whenever you close the curtains again I feel like you are giving up."

"But I'm not!" I answered tearfully.

I tried to reassure her that that was not true. I would never give up on her. From then on, if I opened the curtains in her bedroom, I would not close them again unless she asked me to.

THE YEAR THAT FOLLOWED WAS difficult but then, in a manner, oddly uneventful, even though Frankie's health and emotional situation remained problematic and precarious. Our family doctor referred us to a psychiatrist at the Centre for Addiction and Mental Health (CAMH) on College Street. Our initial meeting at CAMH was in a small room behind a glass partition where a team of three medical professionals — presumably all psychiatrists — observed us and listened to our story. We had been told this would happen in advance. The doctors, whom we could not see through the partition, are so indistinct, so generic, to me now, it's as if they had never existed. We were interviewed together as a family and then separately — the two parents together and then Frankie by herself. We dutifully recounted everything that had transpired with Frankie until then — health history, emotional issues, family dynamics, our theories as to Frankie's depressive episodes.

We then were assigned to be under the supervision of Dr. A at CAMH, a very gentle, young doctor with a slight Middle Eastern accent and quiet, friendly manner. Frankie was to have individual sessions with Dr. A on a weekly basis that would be concurrent with her youth counsellor sessions.

These sessions were unsuccessful. Frankie clammed up and had virtually nothing to say to Dr. A. She felt profoundly uncomfortable with this man. She could not pinpoint why except to say, "Mom, he's *so* awkward, he's *so* shy." His reticence just seemed to stoke her own. She tried two or three sessions and then said she was not in need of his assistance. The doctor told us that Frankie was intelligent and thoughtful, but seemed to have little to say during the sessions. She had something to say all right, she just couldn't say it.

We also talked about medication for Frankie's depression with Dr. A. We, her father and mother, said we were opposed to it. Dr. A was mildly surprised and asked why. I thought this was an odd question. What parent wants her child to be on medication? He didn't push medication and we didn't pursue it. Perhaps he was surprised as medications likely had assisted many other patients he dealt with. I finally told him that Frankie did not want to come back for counselling. The doctor agreed to this as long as she saw someone she was comfortable with, such as the youth counsellor Teresa whom she had been seeing on a weekly basis. Frankie agreed that she would continue to see the counsellor at Delisle.

Then, within a few months, she wearied of seeing Teresa as well. She kept making excuses when it was time to go to her weekly appointments uptown — she didn't feel well, she had nothing to say, it was boring, she didn't need the sessions, she had said everything she wanted to say, she had another commitment, she was too tired. The usual teenage excuses, I thought. This was Frankie's way of saying no or demonstrating opposition to our wishes — just not showing up either physically or emotionally. It was, by now, a well-known avoidance strategy.

Teresa was very amiable and direct with me. If Frankie did not see the value of the sessions and refused to participate, there was no point in forcing her to come. This felt so very wrong, but I could not compel Frankie to go to these sessions. We tried somewhat retributive responses to her non-participation in activities. Not well enough to go to school? Well, that sleepover was not a possibility either. Too unhappy to go to a family event? Then going out with friends was not an option. I wish I could say it improved her behaviour. It did not. At all. It just felt mean and vindictive on our part.

Flash forward to a year later. Things still had not improved and we again were referred to another psychiatrist who operated out of Sunnybrook Hospital in North Toronto. We had waited six months for an appointment. Frankie adamantly did not want to go. Again, her performance was quietly brilliant with this man. He deemed her well enough to proceed without medication or any kind of ongoing psychiatric treatment. In his estimation, everything appeared to be relatively fine and she did not require the services of a psychiatrist.

# A Girl's Glory

✦

I WAS RELIEVED TO LEARN that things had begun to settle down for Julia, with her parents eventually realizing how precarious her physical and emotional health had become with their opposition to her sexuality and to her relationship with Frankie. The father, Norman, initially seemed more conciliatory than the mother, Kylie, and the parents finally conceded that Julia should receive psychological counselling. To our enormous surprise, and relief, Julia's psychologist advised them to accept Julia's sexuality and her relationship with whomever she wanted to be involved. The parents appeared to try to reconcile themselves to this. The girls settled into an easier, less fraught relationship online. Their spirits lifted. The mother ceased trying to communicate with either Frankie or me in a hostile manner.

We started to get to know Julia openly — communicating on FaceTime and Skype. I grew to like her a great deal. She was sweet, intelligent, big-hearted, lovely both inside and out, and I understood how Frankie had come to love her so much. The girls very much wanted to meet and because they were so young, they couldn't do it without our assistance. We began to form a tentative plan to meet in a city halfway between our two towns, but that plan was months away and there was still the school year to get through and more changes ahead.

IN THE FINAL MONTHS OF grade nine, Frankie made a dramatic decision to change her appearance. She decided that she wanted a totally different look. She would cut her long, thick hair very short above the shoulders, a bit like Jean Seberg with curls. Why did I feel such trepidation about this decision? It felt like the beginning of something momentous — something big and significant and a bit frightening. It was more than a mother's blues when her kid cuts her hair, signifying that she is growing up. Did I sense what was ahead?

I took Frankie to my hairstylist Diana — in a small salon in the chic, upscale neighbourhood of Yorkville, but without the Yorkville attitude. Diana looked at us. "Okay, but no tears," she warned in a stern manner. Frankie said with surprise, "But I'm not going to cry!" Diana replied, "Oh, I'm not worried about *you*, dear." She was right. The copious tears that followed were mine.

Diana carefully washed, combed, and braided Frankie's beautiful, long hair and cut it off at the nape. She bundled it up in a neat little package. Frankie had decided to donate it to a salon that prepared hairpieces for cancer survivors. Frankie was exhilarated — she loved it and we did too. I'm sure Frankie saw it as a sort of liberation, as girls and women often do when we drastically alter our appearance. Yet why was

I so fearful? She was growing up and growing away from me, becoming more independent. Rob and I were no longer the most important people in her life. Julia was. This was all normal and healthy and as it should be, but still heart-wrenching for me.

How I longed to bundle up this lovely, fragile child so that nothing would ever harm her. The physical change in Frankie made me melancholic. I approached it with a kind of fore-boding of what was to come. I somehow knew this was the beginning of something much bigger than a hairstyle change. Her life, I felt, was about to change, drastically. It terrified me.

SOMETHING CURIOUS, BUT NOT ENTIRELY unexpected, happened after Frankie cut her hair short and then, even shorter. Each trip to the stylist resulted in a shorter and shorter haircut, much to my chagrin. Sometimes Frankie would return from the hairstylist with a chastened expression as if the stylist had gone too far and she was displeased with it. At one dinner with my extended family, she kept a hat on, saying she was embar-rassed by the cut. I feared that was not truly the case. I felt she had a hand in this new look, but was too timid to say so. Some-thing was at work here but I didn't understand what exactly.

She was right to be a bit fearful. Unsurprisingly, hair is a potent symbol of sexuality and gender in all societies, for all classes. How a person wears her hair says something significant about her to society at large. We are particularly propri-etorial about women's hair and the hair of the girls and the women we love. People often appear disappointed when women cut their long hair and especially disapproving when women shave their heads. We pass judgment on styles, colour, or the elimination of hair. Too much hair signifies some-thing — overt sexuality, aggression, otherness. Too little may do the same. We are somehow affronted by the things that women do with regards to their hair. We naively feel very confident that our opinions will be welcomed by the girl or the woman who makes the change.

Frankie's style had changed tremendously over several months — the clothes and shoes were more boyish and her hairstyle made her gender a bit more ambiguous to those who did not know her. She stopped wearing the minimal make-up — mascara and eyeliner — and the black nail polish she wore altogether and removed all jewellery except for her earrings. Did she want to look older? Did she want to look tougher? Did she merely hate the girly look? Was she trying to annoy us and get a response? Check. Check. Check. Check.

When I expressed displeasure at how short her hair was — at times shaved in certain sections. *Et tu, Brute?* you ask. Yes, me too. She'd sometimes reply in a cryptic manner: "I think you *really* will hate the way I look when I'm older then." This was a not-so-veiled allusion to her desire to shave her head completely. Here I exercised the parental veto — no, no shaved heads, not now, possibly not ever on my watch.

Many times, in public, with this new hairstyle she was mistaken for a boy. Initially and ironically, considering what we know now, this often pitched her into a furious or melan-cholic mood when it happened. If we were on the street, she would get curious looks at times — sometimes not unkind but just inquisitive, which is understandable. Sometimes the looks were a little aggressive. People seemed threatened by the ambiguity of her gender representation. (They still are.) Little children might openly query their mothers as to whether Frankie was a boy or a girl within Frankie's earshot. This was frustrating to her, because she was, I now realize, trying to pass for a girl even though she felt like she was something else inside.

I could not begin to explain this to her without risking a huge fight. To a stranger, *if it walks like a duck and sounds like a duck* — it's hard to lay blame on someone for honestly making the mistake as long as they were not rude about it.

This episode in Frankie's life startlingly hit a personal nerve for me. I had inherited curly hair from my father and my paternal grandmother, which I kept long until I was thirteen or so. My mother, tired of dealing with it and trying to tame it, had convinced me to cut it short. She also lied to me and said it would grow back straight, something I longed for and foolishly believed would happen. But my hair was a curly shag of unruly hair — neither falling in pretty ringlets nor ramrod straight as was the popular style then. It was not a pretty sight and not particularly feminine. When I wore jeans or cords to work, I was often mistaken by elderly people for a boy, despite my curves and makeup. This was disturbing *and* enraging. How could they not see I was a girl? It was confusing, distressing, and depressing, because I *wanted* to be pretty, I *wanted* to be feminine.

Now I can more fully understand Frankie's rage — gender identity is so crucial to a person's self-image that if it is questioned it is frustrating, maddening, alienating.

# Pierced

❖

FRANKIE'S REACTIONS TO A MORE feminine appearance sometimes disturbed me, for this was how I was sensing her sudden
decision to cut off the hair for which she was endlessly admired
and complimented. It was the judgey-ness of it. As a feminist — yes, I will cop to that dreaded and much maligned
"F" word — I am constantly puzzled by the reaction of some
people to the display of femininity. This dislike of the feminine, this femme-phobia as it is sometimes described,
perturbed me, as if to present in a feminine manner is to
suggest that one is less, less than male, less than whole —
frivolous, scatterbrained, obsessed with the trivial and the
superficial. As if the amount of lipstick and the height of
your heels defined you, limited you. It touched me personally — was Frankie rejecting me and the more feminine
appearance I presented? Was that was what was behind her
desire to alter her appearance?

People, both men and women, seem so *invested* in what
women do to and for themselves; they seem to feel very

comfortable commenting on it. It's as if they perceive a feminine presentation and makeup as a barometer of the worthiness of a woman's inner being or self-worth. Too much is an issue (slutty, provocative) but none at all is also perceived as a problem (slovenly, not feminine enough). In their minds, does the artifice of cosmetically enhanced beauty equal falsity? Insincerity? Lack of character? Frivolity?

When I was growing up, my mother alternated between admonishing me to "Go take some makeup off in the bathroom" because I had gone too far and, on the other side, telling my younger sister, "Why can't you put on a little lipstick?" because she thought my sister looked too washed-out or tired.

Exhibit A. All the "gotcha" photos of celebrities without makeup in public places, which now constitute a sizable portion of the front covers of gossip rags and website pics.

Exhibit B. The hmv shop in London retailer Harrods' full two-page ladies' dress code tells workers in every department to wear *Full makeup at all time: base, blusher, full eyes (not too heavy), lipstick, lip liner and gloss are worn at all time and maintained discreetly (please take into account the store display lighting which has a 'washing out' effect).* For non-compliance, a previously lauded store employee named Melanie Stark was forced to resign even though she had worked there for five years sans makeup.

The message seems to be that if cosmetics are used at all they must be used modestly when in the public eye. Unless you are selling it or are some sort of a pop star who is expected to tart it up for the public.

But top-ranking celebrities certainly are not immune to

criticism. Someone like Lady Gaga, who builds her image on extreme artifice and theatrics, takes a great deal of heat for her elaborate makeup and clothes but just as much if she dares to appear in public without. As a simple exercise plug in the phrase *too much makeup* in Google and see the sort of remarks you come up with. Not surprisingly, a great deal of makeup on a woman seems to signal trouble with a capital T.

Exhibit C. The Evil Queen in *Snow White*; the depiction of every mean girl in every movie about mean girls (you can tell she's bad — look at the makeup on her!); depictions of working girls in film and photography; the "talentless" starlets who provide gossip fodder for the Internet, print, and television; and women who are perceived to be garden-variety tramps.

And, sadly, women are just as cutting as men in their criticisms, never failing to register their disapproval when a woman does not conform with their image of what women *should* dress like, *should* look like, and *should* or *should not* put on their faces.

Feminism, for me, has always been about breaking down stereotypes and liberating women from roles that are forced upon them by others, male and female. Feminism should equal freedom — it's not about other women conforming to your vision of what women should be — ranging from their complex life choices about marriage, procreation, and career options to simple, frivolous decisions about whether to wear high heels and mascara.

I STAND BY MY THEORY that shoes and clothes dictate female friendships. A high-heel-wearing aficionado will never bond with a makeup-less Birkenstock lover in any substantial way. Women don't roll that way. Yes, we are *that* shallow at times. We just are not that tolerant of each other. Women, who, by and large, do not want to be perceived purely as sex objects or judged solely on their looks, often do exactly that to other women.

Sometimes my husband will catch me in an up-and-down assessment of a perfect stranger on the street: "You're doing it again!" he will admonish. I have to consciously stop myself as I particularly hate to be the recipient of such a recipro- cal assessment. Frankie was experiencing a bit of that now in public, too, as she experimented with hairstyles and clothes.

Female friends sometimes ask me if Frankie was into makeup — as it happens, it was just a dash of mascara and eyeliner. When I'd say no, they *always* said happily, "Oh great!" as if she, and we as her parents, had dodged a bullet. If I had said yes, what would that have said about her and her choices? Would that have been a disappointment to anyone? A provo- cation of some sort?

I see makeup as part of a costume that I put on every day — a reflection of who I am and who I want to present myself as to the world. Is it a mask? Of sorts. But we all wear masks. We all try to project certain carefully cultivated images to the outside world as women: virtuous housewife, serious and politically aware citizen, devoted mother, hottie, career girl, smart girl, an "I-don't-care-about-fashion" girl. For some, my costume may be just a little more provocative than yours.

I wish we would ease up. If we do not wish to be judged purely on our physical appearances and as sexual objects, let's not judge other girls and women by that standard either. That is neither progressive nor *fair* — yet another F word.

FRANKIE'S LOOK STARTED TO CHANGE drastically. Maybe she was more comfortable with herself since coming out. I can't really justify my resistance to piercing when Frankie first raised it. Maybe because I was raised in a conservative, Catholic environment where we believed that only marginalized people got their noses, lips, eyebrows, and underbits pierced. Maybe I am physically squeamish at the idea. Maybe I am too uncool to get the concept. I cop to all of that.

I have to say it was a real shock when Frankie broached the topic of piercing when she was a pre-teen. *Where did this come from?* I was even more alarmed when she unrelentingly persisted in her request. Her father, infinitely cooler than I am, was unperturbed. Not so for Mama.

When Frankie was younger we had had ferocious arguments about dresses. I wanted her to wear them, she didn't. Why was I so insistent? On special occasions I wanted her to dress nicely — weddings, funerals, special days for my mother. I am old school that way, none of this silliness about always being comfortable at all times. Some events require a level of respect and attention and possibly discomfort in one's dress — especially if her grandmother is involved in said events. She also believes in dressing appropriately for the occasion, something she managed to instill in me.

On several occasions, jeans didn't cut it and Frankie was unwilling to look for dress pants. Inevitably the day of the event would come and we would be unprepared and ready to kill each other just before we were due to leave. Finally we reached a detente about this. I wouldn't force her to wear dresses and she would find a suitable alternative to dresses. You could see how this would kill me — the girliest girly girl who ever was.

*Let it go, let it go,* I would tell myself. Why inflict this on her? It was torture for both of us. Stop being so controlling. I was experiencing shades of my mother and her sisters and their domination over their children, especially their daughters. Frankie's style was more tomboyish, a little punk; a very cool style that I could never pull off.

I really don't see myself as a conservative parent, in dress or manner, but the idea of Frankie embracing piercing was disturbing because it signified ... *what*? I had to think long and hard about my objections. I felt I had to have a rational explanation. I hated when I asked for something from my parents that I thought was a reasonable request and was told "no" without any explanation whatsoever.

Just no. *Punto e basta.*

My answer was no, because I hated the thought of people putting Frankie in a category. People like me, I admit with some embarrassment. When a person has a piercing — admittedly this is an old-fashioned point of view — I presume that person to be some sort of a rebel, anti-authority, trouble. Who wants trouble — especially when you're the parent of a teenager?

It was no because she was too young. It was no because — and this I couldn't admit to her — she would look different from me and that alienated me. It puzzled and hurt me that she had no desire to look like me or dress like me. Then again, did I want to dress like my mother? *No. Categorically no. So, cut the kid some slack*, I told myself.

Lastly, it was no because my own mother would kill *me* when she found out and it would be an eternal source of grief.

How I had disappointed my own mother I now acknowledged with some regret and unpleasant memories. I remembered vicious and profoundly silly arguments about certain articles of clothing my mother objected to: the necessity of the wearing of slips (she wanted me to always wear one with a dress); ankle bracelets (she hated them and thought they had a sexual connotation); scarves and makeup (she disliked them on me); too much hair, too much makeup, clinging clothing or clothing that revealed too much. I stormily marched up the stairs to my bedroom to remove the offending article of clothing many times. But did I stop wearing those articles of clothing, that lipstick, those clinging tops? No, I did not. I just employed more subterfuge as a teenager in wearing them. What right did I have to dictate my own child's appearance? None whatsoever.

I weakened. It was important to Frankie. I realized that my objections were as thin and as ephemeral as gossamer. I finally had to admit that my own style at fifteen had alienated and annoyed my own mother exceedingly. I *dreaded* coming down those stairs into the living room and being told to march back upstairs and take off that makeup ... ankle bracelet ... scarf ... lipstick ... skirt ... whatever. I wanted to spare Frankie that humiliation, robbing her of her self-identity. I owed her that.

# Summer in the City

❖

FRANKIE AND JULIA WERE ANXIOUS about getting a chance to meet in the summer. Julia and her biological father, Norman, knew we were going to a certain town close to where they lived for our vacation that summer. The girls wanted to reconnect. Frankie brightened immensely when Norman called Rob on his cell and said he would like to try and arrange a meeting for the girls.

We planned something simple — meeting for coffee downtown so that the girls might spend a few hours together. Frankie was beyond excited. The only impediment seemed to be Julia's mother, who still held reservations about the girls meeting. But the father told Julia he could talk her around. On the surface he was supportive and sympathetic while the mother still seemed intractable on certain issues. She was ready to accept that Julia was gay but she seemed uncomfortable about the two girls fostering a relationship.

We arrived in town on a June weekday. We were to be there for only a few days. Frankie was still out-of-sorts, despite the end of school and all the stresses that that involved; she was listless, depressed, and faintly miserable. She didn't want to leave the hotel room in a fashionable part of the city to sightsee or shop. She wasn't excited about trying new restaurants. She didn't want to go out for meals. I think she was still anxiously awaiting the phone call from Julia's father confirming a time when they could meet. Julia and her father would be driving in from out of town and it would take just under two hours for them to reach the city. Their arrival depended on his being able to leave work on time, he'd said. We tried to carry on in a normal manner until we heard from them, but it was difficult as we all felt tense and uncertain regarding what might happen. In most instances, either Rob or I would remain in the room with Frankie while the other went out and shopped or went sightseeing. Tension pervaded the trip.

We received a call from Norman. He said that he was unable to leave work and meet us in the city. Both Frankie and Julia were crushed. According to Frankie, she had not physically seen Julia since their chance encounter in the park a year or so before. There was no firm plan for them to meet again for some time and the girls were quite despondent. Frankie left the city dispirited and unhappy.

It was not until many months later that we learned Norman had been totally opposed to the girls' relationship and had no intention of bringing Julia to the city to meet Frankie. He was not the ally we had hoped he was.

# One Job

✦

THINGS WORSENED FOR FRANKIE AS she approached grade eleven. She was on the cusp of turning sixteen. Her marks were uneven when she started the school year. Her self-confidence was in tatters. She still suffered from episodes of lethargy, depression, and social anxiety. If I had one more well-meaning parent, relation, or teacher tell me I needed to use tough love with Frankie I thought I would tear my hair out — and possibly even theirs.

How do you get a teenager out of bed who refuses to even move? Who would lie in bed, weeping and apologizing for her inability to get up? Or worse, lay there in a complete state of withdrawal, too weary to fight you but too depressed to get up? I thought our acceptance of Julia would make a significant difference to Frankie's emotional wellbeing. It helped to a certain extent, but it could not remedy everything, despite our efforts to be understanding and compassionate.

We had discussed the possibility of medication for Frankie. All three of us — Rob, Frankie and I — had been strongly opposed to it. As her parents, Rob and I wanted her to develop her own internal coping mechanisms to deal with these emotional issues. We didn't want her to rely on medication. We had tried for two, almost three years, to manage the situation on our own. Finally we conceded defeat. We could not overcome the situation on our own. We had tried for four years and things were only moderately better, if at all.

It was Frankie who came to me and re-broached the issue of medication. She was exhausted. She was unable to cope with everyday issues and problems. She hated the bouts of crying and inability to rouse herself in the morning, her withdrawal from social life, and school activity. Her lack of interest in all the things she loved — music, hockey, family — was deeply disturbing. She was painfully ashamed of her grades when she knew she could do much, much better.

We, as her parents, felt this enormous weight on our shoulders that we could not speak of openly to others. When we spoke amongst ourselves, it often ended in tears or recrimination, and broke down amongst the same divisive emotional fault lines — one parent was too lax and not demanding enough (me), one was too insensitive (him), and Frankie wasn't trying hard enough (we both secretly feared).

I still could barely acknowledge the word to myself — depression. My child suffered from depression. I had suffered through major bouts of depression myself; I had witnessed people close to me suffering from it — sometimes silently, rarely discussed or acknowledged by the people around them. I felt enormous guilt — had I bequeathed this suffering to her? I sat at my desk at work and cried surreptitiously on the days that she lay in bed unable to meet the day's challenges. Or I would sneak off into the ironically named wellness room in our office — where my coworkers and I often went to make emotional phone calls to family or cry as we had little privacy in our offices — or to the bathroom and weep. Rob suffered through day after day, trying to focus on work in his home office — it was more difficult for him as he was in the same house as Frankie. I confided in almost no one about what was happening because I was bewildered and frightened and angry with everyone. Angry at myself for my inability for help her. Angry at Rob for, I felt, not being compassionate enough. Angry at the poor and ineffective advice I received from medical professionals and teachers who were trying to help me. And, illogically, shamefully, angry at Frankie for being ill.

I debated taking a leave of absence from work to care for Frankie full time. I discussed this possibility with human resources at my place of employment. They expressed sympathy and flexibility. But I feared that my temporary leave would give Frankie an excuse to give up on school, to give up on living, to become a permanent invalid. The idea that I was somehow enabling her horrified me. In the end, I decided against this but explained the situation to my manager and asked for some leniency. I told him that on some days I would be away, some days I might be late, but that I would deduct all of the time from my vacation.

I decided that our reluctant attitude to be open as parents was foolish and dangerous for Frankie. This child was suffering deeply and I was determined to get her relief. I was becoming angry with myself for concealing the true nature of her depression from the school and from those who might help her. My shame at my inability to help my child was getting in the way of finding relief for her. Over a period of weeks, we resolved to take action.

I went to her family doctor and explained the situation, with Frankie present. I asked for the lowest dosage of whatever it might take to alleviate her depression. After a long discussion of her emotional history and a private consultation with Frankie, the doctor prescribed a very low dosage of a selective serotonin reuptake inhibitor — the ubiquitous Prozac, to you and me.

I contacted her school again and explained openly, in detail, to the new vice principal what she had been experiencing. The VP was wonderfully kind and compassionate. I brought in a doctor's note. I wrote individual, personalized notes to each teacher, explaining that we needed them to be patient because of Frankie's illness. Frankie was not absent because she was malingering but because she was depressed. She would complete all assignments, exams, and tests. She would honour all commitments; we just needed a bit of extra time to do so. A couple of the teachers neglected to read my personal note — or perhaps they ignored it — and made some injudicious, sarcastic remarks to Frankie about her absences and late submission of homework.

I felt like my head would explode when she tearfully repeated what the teachers had said to her. Rob, very calmly and judiciously, stepped in and called those teachers personally. He reiterated politely, but firmly, what my note said.

He told them they were free to grade Frankie in any manner they deemed fair but they were not to question the authenticity of her illness. *Ever.* I found myself uttering these five words repeatedly like a mantra: *Nobody messes with my kid.* And I damn well meant it. You want to see a Mama bear in action, you've got it. I kept telling Frankie: "You have one job: keeping going. Don't give up. We will take care of the rest."

# If 1 Was Your Girlfriend

✦

THE SITUATION STARTED TO NORMALIZE for Frankie and Julia. Julia's mother Kylie had come to accept the relationship somewhat and permitted the girls to correspond online. We, the parents, became Facebook friends — surprisingly, considering our initial traumatic introduction into each other's lives and my efforts to block this mother's initial interrogation and harassment of Frankie on Facebook. Julia's mother had consented to a reunion for the girls and we agreed that we would travel to and meet in Julia's hometown. We were to fly to a nearby city, then take a train to their village by the water. We would stay at a hotel in a nearby larger city and the girls would meet daily when they could.

A few weeks before that trip, Frankie came to me with another revelation. How I had started to dread these moments. Each new discovery threw me into an emotional tailspin. Frankie had something to tell me. I girded myself. Here was the truth: the girls had never met at summer camp. They had never met, period. They had met and fallen in love online. Oh boy. I listened silently, trying to conceal my fury. They did indeed have a mutual friend whom Frankie had met online — that much was true — but Frankie and Julia had only ever corresponded on the Internet. Frankie had come out to her friends and Julia had come out to hers, so the mutual friend thought they should connect. Frankie reminded me of a crucial detail she had once told me: she had pretended to be a boy online, while still presenting as female.

I fumed. I had spent thousands of dollars on flights and accommodations for our future trip to meet a complete stranger. We had endured the tension, fear, and anxiety of Julia's mother's homophobic fury when the two girls had not even met. Knowing Frankie's anxiety about the upcoming trip, I swallowed my bile, with a great deal of effort, and went straight to Rob to tell him — letting loose in a manner that I felt I could not do with Frankie. I was beyond furious. Frankie was penitent, she was regretful, she offered to help pay for the trip. But I felt that I had given birth to a very accomplished liar and that was not a pleasant realization.

Now that I have perspective, I understand Frankie's fear and her need to conceal the truth. I don't condone it and it still angers me when I think of it today, but I do understand it. Frankie felt desperate, distraught, in that hormone-fuelled teenager-in-love sort of way that I completely relate to. She would have done anything, *anything*, to see Julia. I'm sure she could not even begin to imagine the initiation of a truthful discussion with me: "Mom. I like girls and I'm in love with someone I met online. Are you okay with that?" From experience I know that a desperate teenager is a terrifying thing to behold.

Luckily, the trip in June was a success. The girls were ecstatic to meet. We had travelled by train an hour away from our holiday location to Julia's hometown, and as we exited the train station, Julia was there to meet us with her mother. The girls rushed together and embraced, openly and unabashedly crying. It was like a scene out of a movie where the lovers are reunited after a long absence. I was struggling to remain composed and not intrude on their moment. I liked Julia very much right from the start — she had a sweetness and gentleness that very much appealed to me. The mother hung back too and gushed at how sweet the girls looked together. She had undergone some sort of transformation. Perhaps she realized how important Frankie had become to Julia, how much they needed each other emotionally. This surprised me but I thought, *Be generous, try and get along, this is important to Frankie and I'd rather perceive this woman warily as an ally than an enemy.*

The town was pretty, bucolic, an hour or two away from a major city. It sat on a bay and reflected small town comfort and modest expectations from life. The locals appeared friendly and open. This was not Toronto — diverse, sometimes chaotic, driven, tolerant of a great deal (some might say cold and indifferent to a great deal). How would Julia fare in this town as a young gay woman? I remembered clearly Kylie's taunts when she discovered Julia was gay: "None of your friends will want to be with you, none of the girls will want to change in front of you at dance competitions." She had threatened to remove Julia from school.

Perhaps things would work out, I hoped. Rob looked at

me in a resigned way, a bit defeated, a bit melancholic. Was this meeting a recognition of something we could no longer ignore — our child was gay? Our child was not what we thought she was initially? Why was this so perturbing?

We went back to Julia's house, which her parents were trying to make ready for the upcoming nuptials of the mother and her new partner, Liam; he was a great person with a friendly, open manner. The mother made a considerable effort to be friendly and the prospective stepfather was very agreeable. We were all civil. That night we were to watch Julia in a dance recital in a nearby town, a multi-hour extravaganza organized by the mother's dance studio. Frankie was excited to meet Julia's friends.

When the girls parted that night after Julia's performance, there was a hurricane of tears and avowals as they made their anguished goodbyes in the dance recital hall — Julia in her colourful tutu and theatrical makeup (she looked like a melancholic fairy) and Frankie in her boyish jeans and hoodie. Much to Frankie and Julia's distress, we could not stay for the entire performance as it was several hours long. We still had to catch a taxi then a train back to the city where we were staying. Frankie wept silently on the train ride back to our hotel, head bowed, eyes unseeing and red. She would not speak or interact with us and was inconsolable in her distress. Nothing could ease her unhappiness except for the thought that they would one day be reunited.

MONTHS LATER WE WERE PLANNING a trip for Julia to come to Toronto in the spring. And although Julia's mother had come to accept the relationship, the biological father, whom I can honestly categorize as a duplicitous and dangerous fraud, was a different story. He was now in the background fomenting trouble like a villain in a silent movie, practically twirling his black moustache, as he strove to drive the two girls apart by whatever means he could.

Julia's biological parents had been separated for some time and the split was not amicable. In fact, it was downright ugly. Norman, Julia's father, was trying to draw Julia away from the mother and gain full custody. Spying on Julia's social media and her texts, he learned of his daughter's imminent trip to Toronto and set the wheels in motion to cause trouble.

Norman went to their hometown's child protection agency with stories he'd concocted about the girls being emotionally unstable and drug users. He alleged the girls were planning, online, to get high, snort cocaine, and smoke marijuana when Julia came to Toronto. What teenager uses the word *marijuana* today? Both girls had sought psychological counselling and he was trying to paint them as therefore unstable. He was actively trying to prevent the trip and malign the mother as well so that he might win sole custody of Julia. None of his stories were true. None were believed — not by Rob, me, or Julia's mother and stepfather. Kylie called me and we discussed the situation. The man was so foul, so damaged, that he was willing to destroy Julia's relationship with her mother in order to get his way. If he wrecked Frankie's life, that would be an added incentive, it seemed.

It did result in one positive result. Julia's mother and I were united in our determination that he would not succeed.

# She's a Girl With a Problem

✦

IN THE FALL OF 2012, Frankie entered grade eleven. It was a month before she would turn sixteen in November. Things were still difficult; things were still not right. We were no closer to the source of her anguish than we were when this all started three years before, after Quinn broke up with Frankie and she went into a downward spiral of despair and anxiety.

Frankie said to me that there was something important she wanted to discuss. Frankie and I were grocery shopping on a cool October night and had just got back into the car. She seemed nervous, but I couldn't surmise why. We were sitting parked in front of the No Frills in our neighbourhood and buckling up. She had a complicated story to tell and wanted to speak to me before she spoke to her dad about it.

She said for months she had been wearing a binder. (Binders are constrictive undergarments used to flatten breasts.) She'd secretly purchased it through a friend's sympathetic mother online, but Frankie needed a new one. (Is that why this woman had said to me, "Our children are special" in a kindly manner?

At the time, it had seemed odd.) I thought Frankie's request was a bit disturbing. Why would she do that, I wondered? Why did she want to wear a binder? She wanted me to purchase a new one for her. I was a little perturbed at the perceived implications of this but I said, "Okay, I can do that for you. If that's what you want."

This request told me that Frankie was profoundly unhappy with her body and was trying desperately to hide her increasingly feminine shape. This explained the heavy sweatshirts she had worn during our typically humid Toronto summer a few months before. Her attire had mystified me; she looked so uncomfortable and I know she hated the heat. I had asked her to wear something lighter and less stifling, but she had always angrily demurred. Her response was one of annoyance and it seemed aggressive, puzzlingly so. Now I knew why. She didn't want me to know that she was wearing a binder. But she had something else to tell me and she was very nervous about it.

"Can't you guess what I'm going to say?' she asked, looking away uncomfortably.

"No," I asserted in wonder. I had no idea what she was talking about. Not a clue.

"Are you sure?" she asked again, visibly agitated.

A long pause ensued as I sat, mystified, trying to guess what she meant.

"I'm trans," she blurted out.

I felt I had been punched in the face. I sat there stunned, shaken. *This* I had not expected. I could not wrap my head around this. How could I have not seen this? I was speechless — I was completely at a loss.

Slowly, Frankie began to explain that she had felt like this for a number of years. Perhaps the very first instance of this realization for her had been a family holiday we had taken with Rob's extended family to the Dominican Republic several years before. Frankie said she had been swimming and was wearing a one-piece bathing suit. She was looking at herself afterwards in a mirror in the hotel and then suddenly she raised her arms and pumped them like a body builder to look at her muscles. She said that she thought to herself, "That's odd, that's like something a boy would do." And she told me different snippets of things that had triggered her realization that she was trans. I listened quietly, trying to take it all in.

I told her it was okay, that I loved her. I'm sure I hugged her, although my mind has gone blank as to what exactly I said and did after this revelation. Some things began to make sense. Her anger about wearing dresses, her displeasure about people telling her she was pretty, her dislike of dolls, her gravitation towards some activities that might be perceived as boyish pursuits — hockey, guitar, photography, all of these were her father's interests, none of these were my interests — her desire to appear more masculine in appearance, to cut her hair short, to stop wearing makeup and jewellery, her tentative suggestions that she was unhappy with her name.

Weeks later, she broke my heart when she burst into tears and said, "I tried to be a girl, Mom. I tried so hard." The next few days were an absolute blur as I tried to formulate how I would tell Rob. I felt shell-shocked, terrified. What would it mean for Frankie for the rest of her life? My life? I knew we would never be the same again.

Two days later, she went up to the safety of her bedroom and, with Frankie's permission, I told Rob as we prepared dinner together. He listened quietly and was very gentle, very accepting in his response, much to my relief. I called Frankie to come down and talk to her dad. She did. He hugged her and reassured her very calmly and gently. Then the three of us hugged. We held her like we would never let go.

I told her we were on her side and I would never force her to do anything she didn't want to do. Later, perhaps weeks later, Frankie told me this: she said she knew it would be all right between us based on something that had happened a few months before.

We had been watching some awful reality program where they set up this phony conflict between two people in a public setting and film the observers' reactions to the scene and then talk to them about it. The scenario was this: a teenage boy sits with his mother in a restaurant booth and starts to tell her that he wants to wear girl's clothes. The mother loudly starts to abuse and humiliate the boy, so loudly that the other restaurant patrons can hear her. The camera trains on the other patrons, some of whom come to an angry defence of the boy. The boy silently takes the abuse. I remember this TV show so clearly because I started crying and said out loud to Frankie, "Oh that poor boy! Why can't she leave him alone?" even though I knew the event was staged. It was so difficult to watch and I remember the boy's face was particularly poignant, very well acted. Frankie had such a kind, loving expression on her face as she consoled me, her arms around me.

I understood painfully, and clearly, that Frankie's secret had been poisoning her — affecting every aspect of her life, physical and emotional. How to purge her of this now, how to make her healthy again? That was our goal for 2013.

# The Bad Girl

❖

FOLLOWING FRANKIE'S REVELATION, I HAD an uneasy and perhaps irrational suspicion that the idea of being a girl was very daunting, perhaps even terrifying, for him. The public events of the fall of 2012 underscored this for me.

I don't have the heart to reiterate the exact circumstances that led to the bullied fifteen-year-old Amanda Todd's suicide on October 10th of 2012. The details utterly shocked me. The still from a YouTube video that Amanda posted just about broke my heart. She held up a piece of paper that read, *I have nobody I need someone.* I felt physically ill, not only with a sense of anxiety about my own child and his female friends, but for myself. I think I felt more disturbed than Frankie. What was happening here?

Frankie referred to discourse on Tumblr and social media about the suicide. He showed me, at my request, the threads about Amanda Todd. I read perhaps twenty to thirty entries and they were roughly divided into three categories:

The first category I will describe as derision towards

Amanda along the lines of calling her a *suicidal whorebag*. This is the precise wording by one poster. These people said she deserved what she got because she had behaved badly and that they were already sick of the story.

The second category was what I considered mystification and intense anger as to why the suicide of one teen should derive that much attention in the media and from parents and rightfully pointing out that many teens, far less pretty than Amanda, die every day and don't get this recognition.

The category I understood was, of course, sympathy for Amanda; these posters chastised the online haters.

One particularly virulent entry was this: *OMG. She shouldn't have been showing her 14 year old tits to pretty much the whole world. I'm so tired of hearing about her, you SHOULDN'T sympathize for her. Yes, no one deserves to be bullied, but when the cause of the bullying is YOUR fault: YOU FUCKED UP BRO. IT'S YOUR FAULT ALL THE KIDS IN YOUR SCHOOL WERE BULLYING YOU...."*

This is unconscionable, unforgivable behaviour, but I honestly think that living online pretty much 24 / 7 has dulled the sensibilities of kids and adults everywhere who have this kind of exposure to the twenty-four-hour news cycle, Facebook, Tumblr, and other forms of social media. It just doesn't seem real to them — it's like blowing the head off a character in a video game. One kid actually questioned whether Amanda Todd existed, thinking her situation entirely fictitious. How else to explain how one person posted a photo of herself pretending to drink bleach (one of Amanda's previous suicide attempts during this ordeal) and then posting *Look at me, am I Amanda Todd yet?* How else to explain that some kids think she did this so that she could have a Facebook page dedicated to her?

AMANDA TODD HAD BECOME THE bad girl. The bad girl who must be punished. The bad girl who had flashed herself online to a grown man. Anonymous hackers specifically determined that Amanda's chief tormenter was a man in his thirties who was alleged to be a Facebook infrastructure engineer and liked to prey on teenage girls on a teen chat forum. He persisted in taunting her to do more online in the way of explicit material, or he would send out the images he already had to everyone she knew. She had also allegedly slept with her friend's boy-friend. She behaved foolishly, perhaps recklessly. She tried to kill herself — unsuccessfully the first time by swallowing bleach and there were many subsequent attempts. So the bad reputation clung to her even as she changed schools and her online nemesis followed her with threats.

A few years ago I heard a celebrated style maven talking about why women wear sexually provocative and inappropriate clothing. Her take on it was that these women felt that that was all they had to offer. Exactly so, I believe — and I think the same is true of teenage girls who behave in a sexually provocative, sometimes self-destructive manner. I think in many instances they fear they have nothing else to bring to the table, nothing else to distinguish themselves or to elicit positive attention.

But this news about Amanda hit me on a very personal level. For I was the foolish girl who did unpopular and stupid things in high school and was vilified for them — not things necessarily of a prurient nature, but things that inflamed my schoolmates and made me look bad. I made mistakes. I had poor judgment. I got into difficult situations and hung around with a group of people who were considered undesirable. By today's standards these actions might be perceived as fairly tame. In no way did I harm or betray anyone other than myself and my own reputation. I refused to capitulate when criticized. I dug in my heels and refused to heed warnings.

Nothing is more frightening to a young girl than the teenage Taliban that determines you have stepped out of line and deserve to be punished. My schoolmates' weapons of choice were much less malignant, if still perfidious, than Amanda's tormentors — her enemies were too formidable and too numerous. I was not beaten up. I was not cyber-bullied. I was not driven from my high school. But I was excoriated. Mocked. Ostracized. Gossiped about. Excluded. It poisoned my friendships. And, I, too, felt utterly alone, completely friendless, as close friends drifted away emotionally, as teachers and family members recoiled in distaste, as I got deeper and deeper into difficult situations from which I couldn't seem to extricate myself. It was excruciating. Ultimately, it drove me to my decision to leave my hometown and move to Toronto where, free from malignant scrutiny, I lived the innocuous equivalent of a nun's existence for two or three years on my own. But I would be lying if I said that I was not scarred and psychically damaged by the situation.

And I sensed the same critical, venal attitude in some of the teens who were voicing their honest opinions on Facebook and Tumblr about Amanda. So, yeah, it smells like teen spirit and boy does that stink.

# In the Year of Falling Apart

✦

WITH FRANKIE'S ADMISSION, HE SOON began to accelerate his requests to transition from female to male. All his pent-up desires and requests began to tumble out; some were reasonable, some were not reasonable at all in the immediate future. He asked that we consult a therapist about how he might go about transitioning from female to male (FTM). He wanted to receive testosterone injections to enhance secondary masculine characteristics. He wanted to explore top surgery and was scouring the Internet for a surgeon who would perform this. He sent me a link to a clinic he found online that performed this surgery, which completely unnerved me. He wanted to change his name legally on his birth certificate — to shorten it to a more androgynous sounding name — from Francesca to Frankie. He wanted to change all his legal documentation to his new name.

This was all in the weeks following Frankie's birthday in November — he had just turned sixteen — and into the month of December of 2012. For me, the Christmas holidays that year were a long and painful battle to process this new information. Frankie struggled desperately to be understood; we struggled to understand. And here, I confess, I made an enormous mistake about how to help Frankie. It's not that I didn't believe what he was telling me, but I wanted to be sure how to proceed; and, honestly, I had no idea how to do so in a responsible manner.

I do not claim to fully understand gender dysphoria — I don't understand the science of it. I have never wanted to be a boy. I've sometimes wanted the privileges of being a man, but never the equipment. It was an intricate puzzle I had never considered. Nor do I pretend to understand it very well now.

I ASKED MY FAMILY DOCTOR whom I might consult about Frankie's situation. My thoughts then were that I did not want to engage a psychiatrist or psychologist who would immediately plunge Frankie into some rapid transition without careful consideration; I did not want Frankie to become a poster boy for FTM transitioning. My doctor referred me to a psychologist in my area who was sympathetic to gay and transgender people but who, he felt, would not aggressively push Frankie in one direction or another. We lined up two or three appointments for Frankie. As with other counsellors, psychologists, and psychiatrists, this was not a success. When I asked why Frankie did not want to go back to the psychologist, he told me that all the psychologist wanted to do was have Frankie write in a journal and meditate, which Frankie adamantly refused to do. He wanted to transition immediately. This is likely a simplistic and unfair assessment of what the psychologist asked him to do, but it was Frankie's take on it.

Frankie started to regress dramatically in terms of his mental and physical health. He stopped going to school, attending two days a week if we were lucky. All the old physical ailments resurfaced: mysterious pains and aches, insomnia, interrupted sleep, irritability, depression, bouts of crying, and social anxiety. The situation became the worst it had been, with the added pressure that we knew exactly what was troubling Frankie.

Note to self: try not to have your child transition while mom is peri-menopausal and experiencing hot flashes. I didn't fare much better than Frankie some days. I felt like I was falling apart. Literally falling apart, piece by piece. Menopause manifested itself in bizarre ways in the year before and after his revelation; for instance, my teeth. In the space of two years I had gum surgery, a new and expensive implant on the right side of my mouth, and then a new crown on the left side of my mouth. Perhaps it was a coincidence, or aging dental work, but all the ailments seemed to accelerate during this stressful period. I think I was literally grinding, or clenching, my teeth into stumps. My head ached, my jaw ached. I had to consciously remember to stop doing this to alleviate the pain. I developed a mysterious pain in my left thigh that went from a mild flutter to a stabbing pain within months. Extra weight? Inactivity? Who knew?

Six months later, my sense of balance seemed to be deteriorating — I fell twice — once in the early winter and once in the late winter; first, a soft fall on snow and then a hard fall in a deep puddle on the way home after an evening show. As Rob picked me up, dripping from the puddle, I could sense his worried thoughts: *Again?* Then shortly afterwards, I fell down a short set of stairs, tearing the tendon in my left ankle. This necessitated physiotherapy and, down the road, a prospective consult with a surgeon. I was clumsy, disoriented, forgetful, and ditzy at times. I had always prided myself on being organized, meticulous, aware, present, but I was increasingly making many mistakes — small and large — in all aspects of my day-to-day life.

I couldn't sleep well — worry about Frankie and how he would survive in this new persona plagued me. How would I tell my family? Our friends? Our neighbours? My colleagues at work? How would the school react to Frankie's revelation that he was trans?

I think I was fighting Frankie's revelation, despite my open and sincere promise that I would not thwart him. Frankie was fighting his own battle and it had taken a physical toll because he had been in denial. Was my emotional resistance now taking its toll on my own body?

# A Voice in the Night

❖

LATE AT NIGHT, WHILE IN bed, Rob and I often heard a voice coming up, we thought, through the open window in our bedroom or through the airshaft. We were unsure which, initially. It wasn't a frightening voice but usually a rather calm, banal voice like someone engaged in a telephone conversation or the sound of a radio played low. At first I thought it was the young girl next door who would often roar up late at night, dropped off by her boyfriend in his hot car, who was perhaps hanging around outside her house talking on her cellphone and the conversation might be drifting up to our bedroom window. Then I thought it might be the tenant who lived in our basement. Sometimes noise travelled through the vents straight up to our third floor bedroom. Finally, it occurred to me that it was my own darling Frankie, who should have been asleep. But when I went to check on him, he was seemingly asleep, the room dark, no sign of him being awake.

The voice, clearly a girl or woman's voice, unnerved me a bit as I couldn't locate the source of it for some time. This went on for months. I felt somewhat haunted, not in the sense that I thought it was some ghostly apparition as I do not believe in the supernatural, but it was something I couldn't determine the source of and it disturbed me. Our house is more than 125 years old. I often think about the lives that have passed through it, the history of the house, the sorrows and joys it has witnessed.

It reminded me of a comic episode some months before (although initially I didn't think it was very funny). Our home phone rang in the middle of the night. There was no one on the other end. When Rob checked the phone log, he saw that the call had come from our home phone. As we lay in bed, he said to me, phone in hand, in this creepy voice, "And then they realized ... the call came from inside the house!"

"Don't say that!" I responded nervously. "Just don't!"

This caused us to check the house, every room, only to find it thankfully unoccupied by anyone other than ourselves. It left us puzzled and disturbed. It took a long time to get to sleep that night. A few days later, Rob recalled that his new cellphone could be programmed so that if someone left a message, hours later, the phone call would be forwarded to the home phone with a reminder that a call had come through. It issued a soft beep to let you know there was a message on your cell. Perhaps the phone had beeped signifying a message had been left and Rob did not hear it. Mystery solved.

But with regards to this mysterious voice ... later, much later, I learned it was indeed Frankie's voice, talking to Julia hundreds of miles away as neither slept very well. During all this emotional turmoil surrounding Frankie's health, his relationship with Julia continued to deteriorate. On Julia's part, she was unhappy with her home circumstances and their separation from each other.

Their unhappiness was legitimate. The two teenagers saw each other very infrequently, no more than twice a year, if that, when Julia travelled here or we travelled to a spot near her hometown. The teens had little or no money, no means of independent transportation, and no way of seeing each other that did not involve the assistance of their sometimes reluctant parents. Julia's mother was not anxious to foster the relationship; Kylie often treated Frankie with cool disregard, even on a good day. She didn't understand Frankie's situation nor was she that keen on making an effort to do so. She appeared merely to tolerate it to make Julia happy.

Julia's father was both meddlesome and openly destructive towards Julia's relationship with her mother and seemed determined to poison Frankie and Julia's relationship as well. Kylie struggled for child support and to keep Norman away from Julia due to unpleasant behaviour he had exhibited in the past. Julia was under a tremendous amount of stress and struggling to deal with it. Frankie appeared to be the lone voice of compassion in Julia's life. And if Julia was unhappy, Frankie was deeply unhappy too. This affected everything in Frankie's life — appetite, energy level, school attendance, involvement with the family, sports activity, social life, and maintenance of his friendships.

Inexplicably, despite their seeming devotion to each other and her dependence on Frankie emotionally, Julia broke up with him. He was devastated. Perhaps the distance was too great. Perhaps she was too lonely to maintain the relationship. Perhaps there were other factors at work. Then they got back together for a brief time. But Frankie no longer trusted Julia and he broke up with her. It was torturous, as neither seemed able to let the other go.

After I discovered that it was Frankie who had been the mysterious voice we overheard in our bedroom, there were long nights of both Frankie and Julia openly sobbing on the telephone post-breakup. I could hear Frankie's plaintive cries quite clearly in my bedroom. Lying in bed uneasily, I wondered if I should intervene. Whenever I cautiously ventured down to speak to Frankie in his bedroom, he tearfully asked me to leave and refused to speak to me. He also refused to get off the telephone with Julia. The next day he would rehash the gist of the conversation that had lasted for hours. Of course, the next day he was unable to function normally, exhausted, distraught, unwilling to go to school.

Julia did not feel supported at home and longed for a demonstration of love from her mother or anyone around her whom she insisted did not care about her. She felt she had no allies, no support, neither at home nor at school nor amongst her friends. As problematic as her mother was with us, I did not believe that Kylie did not care for her daughter. I know she did. On one occasion Julia was particularly distraught and I went on Skype with Frankie to talk to her as well, asking her to speak to her mother or her stepfather about the way she was feeling. *Nobody cares!* she wailed piteously. She claimed she had no one, had nothing to live for. I tried to convince her that her mother did care, as did many others, that we cared, and that she should open up to someone, perhaps a friend or a teacher. We could do little for her hundreds of miles away. She refused and eventually hung up on me, furious that Frankie had alerted me to her distress.

On more than one occasion, Frankie contacted Kylie, whom he was uneasy with, Julia's stepfather, and Julia's psychologist, to intervene as he feared for Julia's safety. Although Rob was personally mystified by all the teenage drama and absolutely wanted no part of it, I was familiar with it and somewhat sympathetic. But I had virtually no impact on relieving either Julia or Frankie's suffering.

Eventually the two parted — reluctantly, dramatically, fitfully, tortuously — as almost all teenagers in love do. But I think they were marked by the intensity of what they had experienced and the barriers they had to surmount together.

# Where Your Children Are

✤

WHEN I WAS GROWING UP in Hamilton, at a certain time every night, a Buffalo, NY television station would intone in an ominous voiceover: "Do you know where your children are?" It sent a shiver down my spine when I heard that question — the thought that a parent would not know the whereabouts of her child, have no sense of what he was doing. But now, I was exactly in that position. I had only a floundering sense of his true state of being. I had been deceived, or unaware, or blind, to his true identity for so long I could no longer say.

ONE THING THAT CAME OF Frankie's revelations was his intense desire to secure the path to a successful and quick transition. It was Frankie who sent me a link to the Gender Identity Clinic at CAMH and it was Frankie who insisted we contact the clinic. The clinic provided psychoeducational sessions to families upon referral from a doctor. I was leery. By making this call, I was making a commitment to supporting the transition. I was afraid of what was to come. I feared I lacked the moral courage to proceed.

I left a long rambling message over the holidays in the winter of 2012–13 on the answering machine of the clinic. I did not hear back until late January. The head of the clinic, Dr. X, contacted me directly, at home, in the evening. We had a long and detailed conversation about Frankie's symptoms, his intentions to transition, our feelings about it, how long he had been unwell, how urgent his treatment was. He also spoke to Frankie to ascertain that we had his permission to proceed. When I hung up, I felt I had not communicated how dire our situation was, how terrified I was about how to proceed. I followed up with a simple, short email saying that we were in serious need of his assistance and I hoped that I had communicated that in our conversation.

In February we received a mound of paperwork in the mail; it requested the medical and psychological history for all three of us. Medical issues, emotional issues, personal family histories, current emotional states. We mailed it back dutifully and awaited the verdict. We were then summoned to CAMH for interviews — together, and separately, by Dr. X and his team, mostly young women, graduate students who were half my age, which was a little disconcerting. We told our story again and again. I was immensely grateful as they had pushed us up the waiting list and, soon, Frankie and I would commence therapy while the clinic assessed whether Frankie did indeed have gender dysphoria.

Each time we went to CAMH, I was intrigued by the diverse roster of children, teenagers, and parents we saw in the waiting room — highly affluent-looking WASP types, smartphones in hand and absolutely no expression on their faces to betray their anxiety; non-English speaking immigrants with a very young child who was literally playing with blocks in the waiting room; stern-looking black moms, obvious business professionals who looked like they'd brook no insolence; Goth-looking teenagers with very plain, bewildered look-ing parents who didn't interact much with their kids. When the doctor opened the door to let us into the meeting room, I certainly felt we were no longer in known territory.

A FEW WEEKS AFTER WE started the therapy, Frankie came to me with some news he found disturbing through his net-work of new trans and queer friends online. Some time ago, Dr. X had been accused by members of the trans community of conducting conversion therapy on young children who had come to CAMH and indicated they were trans. Specifically, the accusation was that he insisted that feminine boys who identified as girls not engage with feminine-oriented toys such as Barbies. This therapy was referred to as the "Drop the Barbie" strategy by one accuser. It required a strict enforcement of traditional masculine behaviour in DMAB (designated male at birth) boys. The allegations go back at least to the early 2000s, according to media sources. Even if this had been true — I cannot confirm it — Frankie was well beyond the age group treated and would not have been affected by this therapy at CAMH.

I can honestly say that I perceived no irregularities in Frankie's assessment at CAMH, but I did find one comment curious that, I think, revealed a flaw in Dr. X's assessment of Frankie as a trans boy (female transitioning to male). Dr. X and I were looking at the photos he'd requested of Frankie covering the years from birth to the present. There was a brief period just before Frankie came out as trans at sixteen when he was presenting in a very feminine manner — girlish hairstyle, some light makeup, pretty clothes, jewellery. Dr. X had been explaining to me Frankie's dysphoria was a bit anomalous — it did not exactly fit the usual pattern of a trans boy coming out. This is the common stereotype of the little child at a very young age who says to their parent: "When do I get to be a boy/girl?" Frankie never experienced this, although some children do.

Dr. X held up a photo of Frankie in a dress. Frankie looked beautiful, admittedly. He said to us, "When I look at this I see a pretty girl." It was as if he was offering it up as proof. To me, it implied that Frankie's trans identity appeared uncertain, perhaps what would now be described as genderfluid. But even I understood then that this was flawed reasoning. Because the external package — Frankie's prettiness or very feminine presentation — did not correspond with the internal gender identity — a masculine gender identity — did not mean that the gender identity was not valid or accurate.

When I am asked about Dr. X today, and there have been many questions about Dr. X in the media and among the transgender community, I can only answer in this way. It's as if he came by and helped me out of a ditch. Later people might have told me that they believed that he did someone else harm; I can't testify to that and I'm not saying it didn't happen. I can only write that he helped me out of a ditch and alleviated a great deal of suffering for all three of us in a time of turmoil.

# My Heart is a Volcano

❖

I STRUGGLED TO UNDERSTAND FRANKIE'S revelation about being trans. I argued with him. I questioned him on certain assertions. I challenged him. I posited different scenarios for him — what would you do in this instance if you were threatened physically? What would you do in that instance? How will you be safe? I feared for his future, his health, and his safety, and, selfishly, ours as well. The things he said haunted me.

"I can't see myself in the future. I can't see an image of myself at all. I can't see myself as a woman or a man."

His words tortured me.

He actively disliked the way his body looked, that he was not tall, that he was not lean and muscular like a boy. Although he is slender, he has soft, round curves like a girl. His language was worrisome. I was very aware of what happens to transgender kids who don't receive support from home and school and how desperate they can become.

Trans kids are more likely to experience peer violence and bullying, more likely to be discriminated against in housing, employment, health services. They are more likely to be homeless than other teens. They are more likely to experience mental health issues and to attempt suicide. They are more likely to be on social assistance.

As Frankie was going through his CAMH evaluation — interviews, questionnaires, medical forms — I was also dealing with my own mother, who was recovering from major surgery. I was making out-of-town trips one night out of three to be with her. We three siblings, my brother and sister and myself, were taking turns caring for her around the clock. My mother couldn't sleep well because of her surgery, which meant that none of us could sleep well when we stayed the night with her. Mom was largely immobile, in pain and not very happy, although she was recovering at a respectable rate befitting the tough old bird that she is.

My nerves were frayed. Two of the most important people in my life were not doing particularly well — Frankie and my mother. When I'd pack up my bag in readiness to drive over to see my mother overnight, Frankie sometimes mournfully would say, "I need my mom too, you know!" Frankie was still having trouble waking up after difficult nights filled with insomnia, interrupted sleep, and bad, ominous dreams that frightened both him and me. On the days that he slept in and was unable to go to school, I would call him later in the morning to make sure he was okay, to try and rouse him into a normal schedule of wake and sleep.

One day, late in February 2013, Frankie did not respond to my texts or telephone calls. I called repeatedly, leaving messages that went unanswered. Then my calls became more frequent. Perhaps it was the lack of sleep, or the constant stress and worry, or perhaps it was the small news item the day before that had triggered a brief discussion about teen suicide between Frankie and me, but I started to lose it.

What if Frankie wasn't answering the phone because he had done something to himself? His phone never left his side, not even while he slept. He took it everywhere. I went outside the office building where I work and walked up and down the busy thoroughfare on Bloor Street West, somewhat frantic. I called Rob. I burst into tears. I asked him to go home and check on Frankie, because he now worked closer to our home than I did. Rob assured me that everything was okay, that likely Frankie was taking a shower, or didn't hear the call, or the phone had died. I begged Rob again to go home and check. I was nearly hysterical. He consented.

He, too, tried to call Frankie and finally got in contact with him. Rob texted me immediately. Everything was okay. I had to calm down. The unmentionable would never happen to Frankie, he would never do that.

I called Frankie back and this time he picked up. Every-thing came out in a flood of anguish. His phone had died and he hadn't seen my calls. I was sobbing as I told him my worst fears. Frankie kept saying, "Mom, Mom. I would never do that. I promise you Mom, I promise I would never do that to you." Then he said he was angry with me for thinking he would harm himself.

But I had reached a breaking point. Anything and every-thing could put me over the edge.

# Meditations upon Concession Street

❖

IN JANUARY 2013, SOME TIME before the incident when I could not reach Frankie on the phone, my sister and I were strolling along Concession Street in Hamilton — the street where the Juravinski Hospital (formerly the Henderson Hospital) is located on what we quaintly refer to as "the Mountain." Concession runs east-west along the perimeter of the Mountain's edge. Our mother, *la Mamma*, was having surgery. That day, like all days involving major surgery, was a case of hurry up and wait.

This was a few scant months after Frankie's revelation in October 2012. I was still reeling from his coming out. My family did not know precisely what was going on; they only knew that Frankie was not well but they could see no discernible reason. As far as they knew he had been having episodes of ill health since 2009, but they did not know why. Why was "she" not in school? Why did "she" miss family occasions? Why was I not more forthcoming about "her" illness? It was "he" and "him" at home, "she" and "her" everywhere else. I felt like my life was spinning out of control — an ailing child, an ailing mother — two of the three most important people in my life were in jeopardy.

Did I talk to my family about Frankie? Oh, hell no. My mother was seventy-eight then and terrified of surgery. My siblings were anxious. I didn't want to add to their anxiety, nor mine in having to reveal the truth. Waiting to be admitted at nine a.m., waiting to be received into the operating room after twelve p.m., waiting for my mother to recover after six p.m., the three of us — my brother, myself, and my sister — gathered with Ma to await the day ahead.

Those who love me might say that some of my more challenging qualities are bossiness, being opinionated, bull-headedness. Multiply that by three and you have me and my siblings. When we were together then — my brother and sister and I — we fell into a somewhat corny but comfortable comic routine meant to distract my mother and ease our anxiety. The routine consisted of bits of our native dialect, and a whole bunch of sarcastic ribbing and gentle abuse.

Away from Ma, we were different. We barked sporadically at each other in response to the most innocuous questions that we assumed the sibling would know. We'd glare at no one in particular, muttering "Don't snap at me," as one of us escaped to get more water for Ma or move the hospital furniture for her to get up and walk around. Immediately chastened, feeling guilty about our bad humour, we would fall into an uneasy silence.

Ma herself was pretty funny, usually inadvertently so. When the nurse asked, "Have you ever been pregnant?"

Mamma mistakenly heard, "Are you pregnant?" "Nooooo," she responded coyly with a smile.

The nurse looked at my brother and sister questioningly. "Are these grown people not your children?"

"Yes, yes," my sibs answered. "We are her children."

The anaesthetist was a sour-faced individual with a hard-to-pronounce East European name who ran through the procedure. He was thorough and clear. "Any questions?" he asked.

"Are there any Italians in the operating room?" I asked. "Well this is Hamilton, I would think so ..." he said dryly, and he departed with nary a smile. The nurse assigned to Ma was very gentle, very sweet, and tried to persuade her to take a sedative during the procedure. But Ma was adamant: she wanted to be fully conscious. Later, in one of the innumerable hallways where we waited, the nurse saw me and assured me that all was well in the operating room. Another very young-looking man came in and marked the leg to be operated on with what looked like a Sharpie. "Make sure you get the right one," I muttered under my breath.

Finally the master arrived, the orthopaedic surgeon, Dr. P, with an ego in inverse proportion to his short stature. He asked Ma what we were doing that day. She said with some amusement, "*You* know what we are doing!"

He did not like this response.

"No. *You* must tell me or we won't operate!" he said, a bit harshly, I felt.

"My hip, my hip ..." Ma replied nervously.

"Okay. Who lives with you now?"

"My mom lives alone," I said.

"No! She cannot live alone after the surgery. She must have someone with her until she recovers."

"Yes, yes. We will live with her until she recovers," my siblings and I answered in unison.

"Good." Then he listed the things Ma would have to do to regain her mobility. "Are you going to ensure she does these exercises?"

"I will try …" Ma said.

"No trying, Missus. Doing, Missus, doing!"

She agreed to everything he said in a sufficiently affirmative manner. And then he was gone, presumably into the operating room to prepare. Ma was rolled away on a gurney to one of the operating suites. She was in good spirits. My sister and I exited the hospital to take a walk. My brother had to return to work briefly. It was cold and rainy, verging on snow. The sky was grey; the street seemed deserted. I was wearing ridiculously flimsy black ballet flats, which got soaked, as I did not imagine that I would be walking up and down Concession Street. My sister and I trudged up and down the street a number of times to get some physical activity in and to relieve the intense boredom we both felt. Then, in need of caffeine, we went in search of a coffee shop, and, finally, food.

We found a used bookstore full of pulp and self-help books in a space so narrow you had to pass sideways through the aisles; a vintage-y and not particularly inviting clothing shop; a dispirited-looking Middle Eastern grocery, where a sullen teenager was stacking mostly empty shelves; and, a small, neat beauty shop that might have served as a location for a film shot in the 1950s. We saw very few people. This part of Hamilton has a smalltown feel. I mean this in a good way. But it also feels like only the old and disadvantaged have remained here and that youth exercised its supple limbs and flit long ago. I had read somewhere that medical services now surpass steel production as the main industry in Hamilton. If the young people are leaving and the steel industry is in trouble, this makes sense. This contributed to my underlying gloom, but there were other things at work here.

To lighten the mood, I commented to my sister on how pleasant the hospital staff were, even those serving the coffee, staffing reception, and cleaning up, which seemed in vivid contrast to Toronto manners in most public outlets. Shortly after this, we popped into a pharmacy on Concession that used to be the site of a well-known banquet hall called the Hillcrest. It was here that my sister tried to get me beat up by a local gal. A rather hard-faced cashier snapped at me, "What are you looking for?" My sister looked me directly in the eye and piped up with, "What do you think of Hamilton now, sister?" I knew this type of woman. I used to be this type of woman. The you-think-you're-better-than-me? type. It's a class thing. We can suss each other out pretty quickly. I knew that the words to the tune in this unhappy clerk's head began with *You are not one of us, chickie.*

She said, rather militantly, "You don't like Hamilton?"

I assured her that I was actually from Hamilton. She softened a bit, and presumably I avoided having my butt kicked. I meet this type of gal often in Hamilton. At the Kelsey's, where my niece was a hostess. In the banquet hall, where my mother's side of the family had their Christmas get-to-gether just the month before. In convenience stores and at gas stations. Those of us who left the city and those who stayed are like rival armadas positioning ourselves in preparation to wage war.

*I should be at home right now*, I thought. I was sick with worry about Frankie. I didn't want to deal with a drugstore clerk with a chip on her shoulder. I had plenty of chips to worry about myself. Real ones, not perceived ones.

My sister and I headed back to the hospital to wait it out in the recovery room reception area. My brother returned from work. We awaited word. We kept checking at reception after hour two, hour three. Exasperated, leaving my brother in the waiting room at the hospital in case we got word, we went out to get some Middle Eastern food across the street at La Luna. We were finally permitted to see Ma in the ICU at six-thirty p.m. They were monitoring her heart; it had been a concern during the operation. She'd had issues in the past with her heart. She seemed drowsy, but was rosy in colour and in good spirits. We perked up, all of us. We texted partners, called children to alert them. "*Nonna* is okay, she's going to be okay." And we relaxed a bit. I relaxed a bit. For a while.

This had been a day of deal-making with the fates. *If the operation goes well, I promise* ... A day of concessions with reality — the so-so food, the bad coffee, the sore back from sitting and pacing. A day of negotiations, ignoring my siblings' dumb remarks in order to keep the peace. It was a day of cajoling, asking the nurse one more time about when the operation would be over. On Concession Street, I also conceded to myself that one day my mother would be gone. I conceded that I, too, would grow old and become somewhat debilitated. I conceded that one day I would be where my mother was and that my child Frankie would likely trod these very same streets in worry, mild boredom, and unnamed anxiety. I conceded that watching my mother in such a state of pain and discomfort made me feel uneasy; I felt childlike in my powerlessness; I was afraid and, shamefully, unwilling to assume the role of an adult. But I knew I had no choice in the matter.

I thought that I would totally lose it — stressed, unable to sleep, angry, and overtaxed. I realize that what I was experiencing was what the vast majority of women my age were experiencing, that some women would call what I was experiencing so deeply "Tuesday." Or any day of the week.

## Una Regina Senza Re

*Povera me,*
*Sono Regina senza Re*

*Poor me,*
*I am a Queen without a King*
ITALIAN SAYING, ORIGIN UNKNOWN

WHEN MY MOTHER WAS RECOVERING from her hip surgery, perambulating about the condo holding on to her walker, she gently started to murmur, "*Povera me, sono Regina senza Re.*"

I asked her to repeat it. Even though I had heard her say it before, I had forgotten it. It was so poetic and so apt. Our mother, as a widow, had enormous influence over all of us. Alone, her suffering intensified the guilt we felt when she suffered or when she was thwarted and didn't get what she wanted. Of course, if she was *la Regina*, we were her subjects and therefore subject to her will.

I have not lived with my mother since before I left for university. Having spent several days with her, alternating with my siblings, while she convalesced from hip surgery, I wrote a blog entry about our time together. I didn't like the tone of what I had written. I wanted to rethink what was at the base of my feelings.

My mother, a septuagenarian, was the designated driver for a posse of old ladies in her circle, many of whom lived in her building. She is active, lucid, social, and sharp-tongued. I hope to be described the same way at that age.

When we're together, fireworks often ensue. She says I am too sensitive and wayward. I think she's insensitive and demanding — but no more so than any of my female relations on my mother's or father's side, young or old. My interaction with Ma usually ranges from passive-aggressive — "People say I am coming to resemble you, Ma." "Really, you mean since you've gained weight?" — to actually aggressive — "Oh, so finally I see my daughter because I'm sick!" she said when I returned for a two-day stay. I have to admit that I am like my mother. As anyone who knows me will say, I give as good as I get.

But in quiet moments, she can be very thoughtful, very tender. She said one day when I was staying with her, "What will I leave behind? Nothing."

I responded in the best way I could. "Us, you leave behind us," I insisted, feeling heartbroken that she felt this way.

"Oh yes," she said with just a hint of resignation, "My children." I reminded her that she has often appeared in my fictional work. She appeared a bit heartened by that.

Another time, as I was tucking her into bed she said in Italian, "*O, c'ho buoni figli ... tutto questo tempo ho pensavo che avevo figli cattivi!*" ("Oh, I have such good kids ... all this time I thought I had bad kids!")

So when *la Regina* came home from the hospital over the

holidays, the heavy emotional artillery came out. On both sides. My sister and I had used all of our two weeks' vacation over the Christmas holidays to take turns caring for her. My brother had done an extraordinary amount of chaperoning her to appointments and doing the legwork getting the condo ready for her return from the hospital. He was staying overnight as well. Each one of us played our part.

The question arose, however, of how to handle the division of labour once she was at home. The nurse assigned to changing her bandages and caring for her at home every two days asked if we had a caregiver for when we, Ma's children, had to return to work. Of course, we had not planned for this. Not because we couldn't think our way through this situation, but because this is how we Mediterranean people roll: we can't have a stranger help around the house. We take care of our own. Even though I lived an hour away, worked full time, and had a child who was going through a major crisis physically and emotionally, I was expected to accommodate this situation, as was my sister — who also worked full time and was a union steward and a committed friend to a number of her circle with health issues. Hiring a caregiver would be seen as a dereliction of my daughterly duty to my mother. As would, apparently, hiring a cleaning lady. My mother said, "Why should I hire a cleaning lady when I have children?" She meant daughters, of course. Sons don't clean house.

I knew exactly what the thinking is behind this. If my sister and I did not take care of the housecleaning, my mother's friends and family would think we didn't care about her, that we had deserted her. It would embarrass her. But I was tired. Exhausted. Near the end of my wits. The very idea of making a trip to another city to clean someone else's toilet stymied me.

Frankie's desire to transition had depleted me emotionally and physically. It was around this time that I had feared Frankie had harmed himself when he didn't answer my phone calls. I was hanging on by a thread — psychologically and physically. But my family didn't know this, nor would they have absolved me from my responsibilities if they had known.

It was at the tender age of ten that I realized that domestic servitude equalled love in our household. After some petty argument with my mother, the issue now long-forgotten, I decided I would sweep the kitchen floor after dinner. It was my assigned daily duty and I hated it. It was simple and could be done quickly; it was an easy task for a ten-year-old, but even then I resented the expectation that it was my job. I knew why it was my job: I was the eldest female child. I felt that my entire childhood was a time of preparation for a life of domestic responsibility.

When I picked up the broom, my mother embraced me and cried out, "You do love me!" I was flummoxed. My sweeping the floor meant *I love you*? That's how I was to show my love? Even at ten, I was shocked at the absurdity of this thought.

Many years after this moment, when she was still in good health and not in need of our assistance, I had a similar argument with my mother. She insisted it was a daughter's role to care for her aging parents. I took the position that siblings should share such responsibilities, regardless of gender. This shook my mother; she was actually distraught and on the verge of tears. "A son can't do that ... a son can't take care of his mother." Likely she was thinking of more intimate care and didn't like the idea of her son helping her bathe. But I remember her shock and disapproval that I did not agree with her view of the natural order of things. Her reaction was like I had almost betrayed her.

And yet there I was, decades later. I was faced with a similar dilemma: was I to pick up the broom — or toilet brush — to prove my love to my mother? Should I? Given the circumstances at my home in Toronto, to whom did I owe my first allegiance?

# A River Runs Through Me

✦

AWAITING THE DOCTOR'S PRONOUNCEMENT ABOUT Frankie's gender dysphoria in the early part of 2013, I felt a sense of dismay when Frankie revealed he wanted to change his name. His birth name was certainly a mouthful. The full name — consisting of the first, middle, and surname — had twelve syllables. "A big name for a little gal," a friend once said when Frankie was a baby.

I chose Frankie's first and middle names very carefully; I love traditional or historical Italian names. Frankie's first name on her birth certificate hearkens back to a Sicilian bandit-revolutionary from the 1950s who serves as a sort of secular saint to this day for Sicilians. He is emblematic of a romantic and impossible goal: the secession of Sicily from the Italian mainland, which he perceived was oppressing and tyrannizing Sicily. He obsesses me still.

Frankie's middle name was the same as my mother's first name — Antonia — which was rooted in imperial Roman history. Antonia Augusta was the daughter of Mark Antony, mother of Claudius — Claudius, the emperor, the scribe, the inspiration for the book by Robert Graves.

I think my choices for names reveal my twin obsessions: bandits and imperial Rome. I am not one to put a lot of stock in mystical experiences with geography or landscapes, but I have had two and they were both in Italy — one in Rome and the other in Taormina, Sicily in 2010.

There was one especially magical moment as we crossed the Tiber River to get to Vatican City at about seven-thirty a.m. The air was misty and silvery and I thought of all the great Romans who had passed over this river: the emperors and empresses, the slaves and warriors, the great leaders of the Roman empire, the ambassadors from other states. When Frankie did not want to take one of the tours, I had to give her a pep talk. I explained that this was the history of her people. She should know what great things the Romans accomplished, the art they produced, the inventions, the lands they conquered, and, yes, that they had to enslave half the world to do it.

When we ventured south to Taormina a few days later, I had a similar epiphany, gazing into my ancestors' homeland, easily the most beautiful place I have ever seen. I could picture bandits and outlaws hiding in the mountainous terrain of the island that had foiled many a *carabinieri*. I felt I belonged there in a way I had never felt before. Despite my pretty little speech to Frankie in Rome, I feel that the Romans are not truly my people, not my true ancestors; my people came from land like this: rugged, wild, dangerous, difficult to navigate, full of secrets like the hidden crags in the mountains.

THE NAMES I GAVE MY child mean a great deal to me. I also understand the need the young have for simplicity, for having a sense of agency about names, and for the ability to choose one's own. But there was for us an added dimension: Frankie was asserting his right to have a male-identified name. Who has the right to control the naming, if not the person who will bear that name? *Frankie — he —* has that right.

I understood Frankie's desire and right very well. At approximately the same age as Frankie was at this point, I decided to go by the much simpler Anglicized form of my name before entering high school. I had endured a number of excruciating years of having people mispronounce, butcher, or mock the name my parents gave me. It did not help matters that the name rhymed with something disagreeable. I was taunted with it.

When I was ten years old I had a particularly obstreperous grade school teacher of Scottish descent. Miss M informed me that I was mispronouncing my own name. She also informed me that I was spelling it incorrectly. *My goodness*, she must have been thinking, *her dumb immigrant parents don't even know how to spell their own child's name!* Imagine the furor today in the Toronto District School Board if a teacher dared to do that.

I never was a fan of my first name, although I retain it on all legal documentation to this day and flirt with the idea of restoring it on a more casual basis, but I knew it had a special significance in the family. It was my paternal grandmother's name — a woman widowed at thirty-four who had raised five children on her own. The first or second daughters in the families of her five offspring hold the same name.

My reaction was swift and tearful when Miss M tried to change it that day in grade five. It provoked a firestorm of tears and resistance. I never complied with her thoughtful suggestion. I may not have particularly liked it, but my name was mine to keep or discard. So, say my name, say my name. Say it the way I want it said. It's my right.

And it was Frankie's right, too.

MUCH LATER, FRANKIE CAME TO me with another request to change his name. The first time we changed it, I encouraged him to make it sound more androgynous than masculine. Yes, I admit that I interceded and asked Frankie not to make the name change too masculine sounding. He was sixteen years of age and at the beginning of his transition. I honestly felt that I — and we as a family — could not handle the questions, looks, and paperwork, when no one outside our immediate family and the circle of Frankie's friends was aware of what was happening, not even our closest family members. I admit I responded cautiously. Perhaps cowardly.

I felt overloaded emotionally and unable to process his multiple requests for change — the possible required physical changes to his body; the pronoun change from her to him; the legal change of names eliminating the names I had given him at birth; learning to use the word son rather than daughter; the desire to use the men's bathroom rather than the women's. I felt overwhelmed and panicky.

I now know that many trans people choose alternative names that often do not denote gender. I have become familiar with this through the new network of friends that Frankie is making. I was grateful that Frankie had chosen to shorten his feminine birth name to Frankie rather than choose an unambiguously masculine name, such as Steven or Marco, that I was unaccustomed to and would struggle with. As it was, at the beginning of the transition, when things got very heated during arguments, I would inadvertently revert to his birth name. This was akin to throwing gasoline on an already raging fire, causing him to flare up even more angrily.

Now I braced myself when he said he wanted to go by another name. He wanted a more masculine sounding version of his name and he wanted to add a middle name. I started to feel angry. I felt, irrationally, that my future already had been taken away from me, my identity as the mother of a daughter was gone, and now the names I had chosen for my child, one by one, were being stripped away as well. I felt proprietorial about his name. His name. As if he didn't have the right to call himself whatever he liked.

"What is the new name?" I asked, trying to mask my anxiety.

"River."

"River?"

"Yes."

"Oh." What. The. Heck. This I was not expecting. I don't know what I was expecting, but it was not this.

"I want to legally change my name to include River as a middle name."

"Oh." I took a long pause while I scrambled for a neutral response.

I admit I disliked it when he proposed it. As I mentioned,

I preferred historical names, family names, names that had a special significance for the parents and the family; like names of bandits and Roman empresses. As I write this now I think about how ridiculous my protests sound. I felt resentful. Why did I have to give up everything about Frankie's past that gave me pride and pleasure?

Instead I said, "Okay, well, let's just think about that."

At this time we also began to have an ongoing argument about old photographs of Frankie that were displayed in the house. Some of them made Frankie uneasy. He asked that they be removed from public display. I felt that I was compromising by adding new photographs to the old ones — a mixture of the past, which I loved, and the present.

Two of my favourite photographs proved to be the most problematic. One was a school picture of Frankie at eight or nine with gorgeous, thick ponytails and a beaming smile of crooked little teeth. Frankie is wearing a bright red top that brings out the olive tone of his skin. I sometimes wondered if perhaps because I had commented on how much I loved this picture, from a time prior to his transition, Frankie had grown to dislike it. Did it sound to him like I was I saying I loved him more back then when he presented as female? Did that irk him?

I could not love him more. But I adored that little girl, too. She was beautiful and bright and fun — and I was mourning the loss of her in my memories. At times, I had a terrible feeling that the past, as I remembered it, no longer existed, had never really existed, and that feeling terrified me. I began to feel that the history I had with my child was an illusion, a pure fantasy; I had had a baby girl, but now it seems I had not. At times I wept inconsolably and bitterly at the thought of what I felt I had lost.

The second was a picture of a picnic gathering when Frankie was less than ten years old of all the females on my husband's side — my two sisters-in-law, my niece, Frankie, and me. I remember a family friend had seen us sitting on a blanket together at picnic, all cozy and laughing, and he kindly offered to take the photo. I could see that he was moved by our gathering of female relations. I loved this one too. A great deal. It's the only picture I have of just us girls together.

Frankie wanted both these pictures taken down from the mantle, my pride of place in the living room. Was it because it was all girls and he no longer felt like one?

I resisted. I thought to myself, *Maybe I can sneak that photo off to my workplace to enjoy it on my own.* But this was a treasonous thought, and I realized that I had to resolve to move the photos to a less obvious place in our home.

EVENTUALLY, FRANKIE DECIDED HE DIDN'T like the androgynous sound of Frankie either. He wanted a more masculine sounding name — that or the name River. Rob, bless his heart, tried to use the names that Frankie wanted. He was largely successful. I struggled.

One time, when I used the name Frankie, our child said, "That's not my name."

"That's not your name? Frankie is not your name?" I said in bewilderment.

"No, that's not my name." He kept repeating that phrase

over and over like a petulant four-year-old. I could feel my head was about to explode.

"Well, that's what it says on your birth certificate now and if you don't like it you can pay another two hundred dollars to get it changed."

"That's rude," Frankie said in a surprised tone.

*Is it?* I thought. *I don't really care.* He was leaving to sleep over at his new girlfriend's house. Rob was to drive him there. We said goodbye curtly and I went up to bed. When Rob returned, he said that Frankie was upset in the car. *Welcome to the club*, I thought glumly. "I don't want to talk about it," I said. But I did. I was just too tired to argue.

Rob said, "I know why it's hard for you to use the new name. You feel like it's the last bit that we have of our old life with Frankie. You don't want to let it go. I was trying to explain that to Frankie. I get it."

But did Rob get it?

I didn't say anything. He was right. That's exactly what I was thinking. Everything else had been taken away. Now I didn't want the name that I had given him taken away too.

# Like a Bomb Went Off

✤

JUST AFTER FRANKIE CAME OUT, I remember saying to a close friend that I felt like my heart was withering. I felt less compassion for those who experienced the daily vicissitudes of life. I did not care if a colleague's father-in-law snapped at her at a family dinner. I did not care if a friend was having trouble finding meaningful work or that my neighbour's secretary was inept. In my ferocious heart of hearts I said to myself, *If you only knew what was inside me, you would never open your mouth again.*

A close friend, who has experienced the traumatic news that of one of his children was diagnosed with autism, told me that this feeling would pass. "You will feel, at the beginning, every day, like a bomb went off. But it will go away. You will feel normal again, because your body will not be able to withstand the stress of that constant anxiety." He told me to wait, to be patient. One day that feeling would disappear.

THOSE WHO KNOW ME KNOW that I am not one who is reluctant to speak about my emotions. But I found the weekly therapy sessions at CAMH quite unsatisfying. Frankie had a session with his therapist and I had a concurrent session with a different therapist. Rob — because he is a man? — felt no need whatsoever for therapy.

My therapist — a graduate student working under Dr. X, the head of the clinic, who could easily have been my adult daughter in terms of her age — was kind, thoughtful, intelligent, and genuinely sympathetic. But there is no way in hell's acre she could possibly understand what I was going through, except on a purely intellectual basis. I was exhausted, frustrated, angry, confused, afraid for my child, terrified of what I should say to family, friends, and colleagues. I often wept during sessions and then wept again afterwards on the way home in the car with Frankie, much to his chagrin. Frankie would ask me what was wrong and I would resist. Then I would stop resisting and tell him my anxieties. He responded by accusing me of making his transition all about me. He said, "I need you to be strong. I need you to be the grown-up here." He was right, but I found these interactions upsetting, uncomfortable, intolerable.

Eventually, I went to the head of the clinic and, as ardently as I asked to be admitted months before, I asked to be released from my weekly sessions with his blessing. He resisted. He felt I needed the sessions. I needed something, certainly, but I had trouble articulating what that was. I presented my case to him as carefully as I could: how could a twenty-something, unmarried, childless person — no matter how compassionate and kind — understand my predicament? There was the issue of the dealing with Frankie's gender dysphoria, his depression, his transition from female to male. There was the strain on our marriage as Rob and I struggled to cope with these ups and downs in addition to the petty ups and downs of daily life. There was the burden of the secret we bore, as I was ready to discuss it with very few people at that point.

I really wanted a forum where I could vent and speak honestly about all my conflicting emotions amongst other parents who understood. I was angry, really angry, about the hand I'd been dealt and even if it was irrational I wanted to talk about that aspect of my feelings. Dr. X seemed to feel that I would not be able to find such a parents' group. The minute he said that I knew exactly what he meant — any parent group would de facto be a rah-rah session for the parents to rally themselves, in a positive way, for the challenges ahead in supporting their children, and not a place to whine about their circumstances and situation. It would be unseemly and unproductive.

In some literature I picked up on this matter, I remember it emphasized how the parent should not be communicating his or her negative feelings about the transition: discomfort, embarrassment, anger, shame, confusion, bitterness, etc. Especially to the child. And yet it is there, my good people, it is there. Now I think how ridiculous this supposition was. How could I continue on as an involved, honest human being without voicing my concerns to my child in a respectful manner?

In the summer of 2013, we were asked to gather and meet with Dr. X. He was ready to give his assessment of Frankie's gender dysphoria. Frankie was nervous, "What if he says no, and we can't proceed?" I reassured him. It would not be completely Dr. X's call, although his assistance would make Frankie's life much easier. I valued Dr. X's opinion, but we were not about to condemn Frankie to a life of misery trying to be something he was not because a medical professional did not agree. I told Frankie, we are on your side, always. I also told Dr. X that. No matter what his medical verdict, Frankie would determine the course of his life, and only Frankie.

When the three of us met, Dr. X told us that in his opinion, Frankie was indeed suffering from gender dysphoria and could undergo treatment — both physical and psychological. There were some anomalies in Frankie's personal history, but he agreed that Frankie was experiencing it. Among the anomalies, he noted that Frankie did not become aware of his gender until a much later stage than many children, and also that Frankie still wanted to have children in some form or another. Dr. X said this was rare. The anomalies did not mean Frankie was not trans, but they appeared to be deviations from the usual pattern of self-awareness about a transgender identity.

The doctor said he would refer Frankie to an endocrinologist within six months, and also advised that he receive monthly injections of hormone blockers, specifically Lupron, to be administered by the family doctor. This would suppress ovulation and the menstrual cycle and inhibit the further development of secondary female characteristics. The course of action would continue for six months unless something unexpected transpired, such as an adverse reaction to the drug.

In six months, if the endocrinologist and Dr. X approved, Frankie then would go on testosterone therapy to enhance his masculine characteristics. This would result in the deepening of Frankie's voice, the growth of body hair, and an increase in muscle mass and strength. Frankie was to continue weekly sessions with his therapist at CAMH.

I also had been referred to Dr. B, a woman closer to my age, which I found to be a relief. I needed an advocate. I needed someone on my side to advise me when my concerns were valid, and when they were not — to determine if my worries were tainted by transphobia or fear or both. I was desperate for objective counsel from a sympathetic professional. I found it in Dr. B.

Frankie wanted to pursue top surgery, but Dr. X said he would not recommend this until Frankie turned eighteen. Dr. X is conservative on these issues and has been vilified for his refusal to budge by some in the trans community. If the diagnosis of a child under eighteen is positive, in that the doctor agrees that they have gender dysphoria, he will agree to start testosterone injections / hormone replacement therapy (HRT) at seventeen and then top surgery at eighteen. There was a paternalistic edge to this assessment that concerned me. During these discussions, I perceived that Dr. X was warning Frankie that if he did not attend school, if he continued missing school in the manner that he did, the procedures would not take place.

In retrospect, I find this approach alarming, although at the time I think I would have agreed to anything that led to Frankie getting the assistance he wanted and needed. There was an element of "If you don't do as I say, I will withhold this medical assistance from you." I did not like the idea of linking behaviour to medical assistance. But as much as I disliked the paternalistic approach, it worked. It gave Frankie a focus and a goal. Nothing else had worked. Neither threats nor cajoling, neither incentives nor rage-filled threats issued by his parents. The promise of the hormone therapy and access to the testosterone made him more diligent about attending school. He wanted hormone therapy, he wanted surgery, and he wanted these sooner rather than later.

Frankie appeared disappointed. He wanted to start hormone replacement therapy immediately. Dr. X wanted him to go slowly. As did I. I thought we all needed time to adjust. It was the summer and Frankie would likely see the endocrinologist in October or November of that year, 2013.

MANY OF THE MEDICAL PROFESSIONALS whom we have consulted over the years ask, appropriately, what Frankie was like as a child. Presumably this would be a key to his present day inner turmoil, or unhappiness. Were there any signs of what was to come? She — as Frankie identified then — was generally a happy kid, a goofy, high-spirited, slightly nervous child who did not have particularly high self-esteem or confidence. Why this was so was puzzling. She was considered to be pretty, bright, and moderately popular, with many friends of both genders. She was nervous in new situations and meeting new people but that just seemed like the nervousness of an only child unaccustomed to sharing with siblings.

Frankie was very playful, fun loving. She liked to be teased and teased people in return. One day a game evolved where I stuffed one of her clean socks from the laundry into the front of her top. Comically outraged, she chased me through the house and had to do the same to me — back and forth we went every time there was a fresh load of laundry, screeching, scrambling on socked feet on the wooden floors of our house until we fell into a heap of giggles on to the couch or nearest bed.

When she was four or five, I bought her a little pink T-shirt with a picture of a monkey and the words *Bad Monkey* emblazoned on it. She was delighted when I started to chase her around the house admonishing, "Bad monkey! Bad monkey!" with a mockingly stern voice and a raised finger of disapproval.

We once took her to the Riverdale Farm as a toddler to look at the ducks. She turned to me and said, thoughtfully, "They're not talking!" Then she resumed her placid gaze into the pond full of ducks and ducklings. Pure goofball.

She often had trouble sleeping, something I think she inherited from me. When Frankie would lie down to sleep, the wheels would start to turn and turn and she would be resistant to sleeping. She woke constantly, crying out, afraid of the dark, afraid of being alone. It didn't help that we had bedrooms on different floors — Frankie was on the second, we were on the third. That seemed to increase her anxiety.

She usually hated big scenes, crowded houses full of chattering relatives, loudness, kids running around the house screaming at birthday parties. Sometimes she just wanted to hide when people came over. But she had a multitude of friends, many of them were little boys with planned play dates and sleepovers. She was often the only little girl invited to an all-boy birthday party that I think was a source of quiet pride for Frankie. And, to be honest, for me, too.

One thing that worried me when Frankie was young was her expressed anxiety that her friends didn't really like her. I couldn't quite fathom why she felt this. She seemed uncertain of the honesty of their regard for her. The only time I really had concern for her, prior to her experience of deep depression at twelve years of age, was a scene that I keep repeating in my mind now. She must have been ten or so and we were listening to a radio or television program (I can't recall which) discussing the fact that mental illness sometimes surfaces quite suddenly and violently in teenagers, perhaps fuelled by hormones and puberty. She was very quiet while we listened. Then at one point, Frankie said very simply, devoid of drama, "I think that's going to happen to me."

I felt like I had been struck. I sat still, barely daring to breathe. I turned to her with all the calmness I could summon up and quietly asked, "Why do you think that? That's not going to happen to you, Frankie." I didn't want to make a huge issue of it, but her statement unnerved me.

She responded, "I just think so." There were no histrionics, no tears. It just seemed like quiet resignation to a future that she perhaps foresaw. She only said this once to me. I never spoke of it again to her or to Rob, or anyone else for that matter, until very recently. When I mentioned it to Frankie a short while ago, he had no recollection of this pronouncement at all.

Sometimes I turned to Rob or to my friends or family in despair and said, "Why is Frankie so depressed? So unhappy? She was such a happy kid." How did I miss this? What didn't I see that I should have seen then? Where was the little girl I had chased through the house delighting her by calling her a bad monkey? The one who ran squealing "Mommy, Mommy, Mommy!" because she was so excited to see me when she came home? Who cuddled in my arms when hurt or sad? The little girl who, when she needed comfort, rested in my arms, her head on my forearm, her small feet poised on my thigh as we fell asleep together. Now, I can only think of this through the lens of gender dysphoria. Something was not right. Frankie knew it was not right and that someday it would surface even if she could not name it.

# In the Men's Room

❖

ONE OF THE FIRST THINGS that Frankie requested once he came out to us as trans was that he be able to use the men's room in public while transitioning. I was somewhat touched, but disturbed, that Frankie asked me for permission. He could have been very devious and done this behind our backs. But this was an issue for me; I said no immediately. It was in the first few weeks of Frankie coming out and I was still reeling from the revelation. I didn't even consult Rob about it. I was adamant. I made Frankie promise — I practically begged him — not to walk into a men's room. He reluctantly agreed, but asked why I was so opposed to it. I said I was afraid for him. I felt that he could not truly pass for male yet and if someone thought he was female they might harm him. There is no shortage of unstable and bigoted out there, I reasoned. The idea truly frightened me. But Frankie argued with me.

"But I do pass mom," he insisted. "Lots of people think I'm a boy. Most people do." I found this hard to believe despite his short hair, boys' clothes and shoes, and piercings. When

I looked at Frankie, I saw something profoundly female. Perhaps I was refusing to acknowledge the truth of what he was saying, perhaps I was blocking out what others saw, but I saw a boyish girl, I did not see a boy. Not yet.

"Your face is too pretty to pass!" I shot back by way of ending the argument. I was not budging on this one.

A few years ago, we three were returning from a family trip to Chicago and while we were in the Midway International Airport waiting for our return flight to Toronto we all needed to use the facilities. Of course, as usual, the lineup to the ladies' room was out the door and down the hallway, whereas there was no lineup for the men's room. Frankie asked his dad if he could go into the men's room with him. Rob said sure. Frankie asked me if he could. I blew up at both of them on the spot.

"Why would you agree to that?" I asked Rob indignantly. "You know how I feel about that. Why are you even asking me that question?" They did not go in together. Frankie was very angry with me on the flight home.

"You said it was about safety. You said you were afraid for me," he said. "But you know that nothing will happen to me if Dad is with me. So you lied. It's not about that. It's about something else."

Busted.

I really could not respond properly to his criticism. The washroom issue is a major hurdle for trans people. If they are nervous about which facility to use, they often simply don't go to the washroom. They wait. They wait until they can find other, more private, safer facilities. This happens at school, in the locker room, in public places. It was becoming a big problem at school and in public for Frankie. It was the cause of tremendous physical and emotional stress for him.

I asked why, of all the issues, we had to deal with this regarding his transition, why this was so important to Frankie. He explained, "When I go into a women's washroom, girls and women sometimes stare at me rudely. Little kids ask if I am a boy or a girl. It makes me uncomfortable and I don't even want to go in there. When I go into the men's washroom, nobody looks at me. They just do their business and leave."

This was true. I had seen the hostile and inquisitive looks he received when Frankie was in the women's room. If I am to be honest, I truly feared this part of the transition. It terrified me. Each day I was asked to go a little further with this transition and I resented it. I feared it. Afterwards, Rob talked to me about my overblown response in the airport. He said, "I thought it would be okay, I thought he'd be safe. You know it's going to happen one day, right? He's going to need to go into the men's room. And you can't control it forever. You know that, right?"

I said nothing. I had nothing to counter this. I would feel safer if he was in the women's room; he would feel safer and more secure if he was in the men's room. I have decided that I am much like St. Augustine of Hippo, a Christian theologian, who prayed to God: "Give me chastity and continence, but not yet." That's how I felt about the whole men's room issue. Give me tolerance and respect for Frankie's transition but please ... don't ask me to do it now.

# The World's Smallest Jean Jacket

✦

A SCANT FOUR MONTHS AFTER Frankie's revelation about being trans, and with my mother still healing from her hip surgery, we got a telephone call from an adoption agency in Ottawa. In Ontario, they mercifully grant a civic holiday called Family Day on the third Monday in February. The call came on the Friday preceding Family Day in 2013. We had commissioned the agency to help us adopt a baby girl from China some years before. The voicemail message said that if we were still willing, the group of ten families that we had signed up with would be leaving for China in a few months to meet the little girls who had been selected for us by the Chinese government. This elicited both shock and despair as we, as a family, had given up hope that the agency would actually come through with the adoption after we had made repeated requests for information and a confirmation of our impending trip. The telephone call threw the whole house, including Frankie, into a state of emotional chaos.

Rob and I, notoriously late bloomers in many key areas of

adulthood, had had Frankie when I was in my mid-thirties.
We really hadn't started planning for the next one until I was
almost forty. This was a big mistake, we learned belatedly.
Everything having to do with conception and fertility becomes
much harder after the mother reaches thirty-five years of age.

We tried to conceive on our own for six months, but to
no avail. We didn't worry too much initially. It never occurred
to me that I would be unable to conceive. We went to a
fertility doctor who prescribed hormone enhancement and
fertility treatments for another six months. This was also
unsuccessful. After a few years of quiet resignation, my sister
Francesca stepped forward and offered to donate her eggs so
that they might be implanted in me and I could conceive and
give birth. I was a little long in the tooth for this procedure
but the fertility doctor was optimistic. The odds he gave
me were good, better than average. Of course, thousands of
dollars were at stake; it was in his best interests to put an
optimistic spin on the possibility of conception. A friend of
a friend had conceived twins with this doctor a short while
before this, but she was a good deal younger than I was.

My sister Francesca journeyed religiously from her home
outside of Toronto to a clinic for her weekly hormone treatments to enhance her fertility and egg production over several
months. She underwent the eventual surgical extraction of
her eggs. I went through a series of hormone injections
to prepare my womb for conception. But despite our best
efforts, the implantation failed. I almost immediately began
to expel the eggs once they were implanted the day of the
procedure.

The day the implantation failed, I stayed home, devastated. Frankie came home from school and could tell immediately I was in distress. Frankie is the one person who knows exactly when I am upset. I broke down and told him the implantation had failed. He guided me to the couch and asked me to lie down and relax. He turned off the lights in the room and told me to be calm, trying to soothe me as I wept my way into another fruitless night of mourning for what might have been.

I remember returning vials and medical equipment to the fertility clinic some days after the procedure and glimpsing, with shock, a coworker sitting in the waiting room. I did not speak to her — she never knew I was there — but she eventually conceived a little girl.

After this, we started to consider adoption seriously. We tried several routes. We contacted the Children's Aid Society and attended a meeting to determine if we were the right fit. I was entranced by the portrait of biracial child they had on a poster then — she had light-coloured, curly hair, much like mine at that age, and light-coloured green eyes. It's a fantasy, I know, but she looked healthy and beautiful and fit the physical ideal of what I had always wanted in a child. When an aid worker examined the questionnaire we had filled out, she politely suggested that, as we had expressed wariness about adopting a child with medical, psychological, or substance-abuse issues, perhaps private adoption would be a better path for us. We agreed. Neither of us wanted the additional responsibility of a newborn or toddler dealing with substance abuse or a physical disability. We felt we were too old, too tired, to do this without resentment.

We went to a lawyer who specialized in connecting prospective parents with young women who wanted to give up their babies. Many of these were Chinese students studying abroad who had accidentally become pregnant. She was very blunt — they often sought Chinese adoptive parents and we did not fit the desired profile for these young girls. She said things could go incredibly well and quickly based on our diverse ethnic partnering for someone who was seeking that sort of match (of European and Asian descent) or it could be a dead-end as it was such an exotic pairing. Exotic? Even in Toronto? I thought, *We are exotic?* Apparently so.

We underwent a multi-hour interview and extensive examination by a social worker who lived in our area and was recommended to us. She was to determine if we were suitable candidates. We were processed by the police department for possible criminal records; we provided financial proof through our employers of economic stability; we got letters of reference from friends and colleagues; our doctors verified that we were healthy — physically and psychologically.

We also signed up on an adoption website and sent photos and a written profile of our family. We reached out to other adoption agencies, hoping to cast the net a little wider. For the next year or so there was nary a nibble nor a query from anyone. We were, perhaps as the lawyer prophesied, too exotic, too old, too perceived-to-be-past-it, to be ideal adoptive parents, although we knew others who were more successful than we were using these same resources.

The final straw in our domestic search was the only possibility we were offered by the adoption lawyer — she had

THE UNFINISHED DOLLHOUSE    143

found a Hispanic mother in the U.S. who had been a drug user and was about to give birth to a mixed-race baby. I wanted to leap at the opportunity, but Rob had a saner point of view. If we were willing to take a child who had possibly been exposed to drugs and alcohol, why would we go to the expense of travelling to the U.S.? Weren't there enough of those children here in Canada through Children's Aid? They needed our help. He was right, of course. We closed the door to that avenue.

In late 2006, as a last resort, we signed up with an agency that specialized in helping parents adopt newborn girls from China. Bear in mind that we had been trying to conceive or adopt since the year 2000. We went to a presentation in a suburb of Toronto and listened to an agency representative who was born in China and had extensive connections there. She seemed to be the perfect liaison with the Chinese government and was highly recommended by our social worker, who was also an adoptive mother. This woman ran the agency with her Canadian-born husband. The emotional clincher at the presentation was a parade of beautiful little Chinese toddlers and girls, who, with their parents, filled the room after the presentation with their enchanting giggles, taffeta dresses, and screeches of pleasure. If we were not sold on the idea before, we were there and then.

There was another round of medical appointments, letters of recommendation from employers and family, and proofs of financial solvency. There was a thorough vetting of criminal records — this time because we were going the international rather than domestic route. This process is harrowing, expensive, and stressful.

Within months we were assigned to a group of ten pairs of prospective parents with whom we would travel to China when we finally received our approval from the Chinese government. The other adoptive families came from almost every province in Canada. Our expectation was that we would be flying to an unspecified city in China within a matter of months. We excitedly told our extended families — some vowed to come with us on the journey. So we waited. And waited. And waited.

By a quirk of fate, a good friend was dating Dr. C, a family doctor who worked in upper New York State. He learned about our dilemma and the long time we had been waiting for a child. He was an obstetrician-gynecologist who practised in a small town near a college. One day we got an excited call from Dr. C saying that he might have a baby for us to adopt. One of his patients was a young academic, an Asian female, living with another academic, who was a Caucasian male. This was exactly the racial mix we had hoped for. She became pregnant and was considering giving up the baby so that she might continue with her academic career. It seemed too good to be true: a mixed-race baby under the care of a reliable friend. He had been talking to the couple and they seemed very disposed to meeting with us. Our hopes soared briefly, but, sadly, in the next few months, the mother miscarried and so yet another path to adoptive parenthood was eliminated.

Unfortunately, the opportunities to adopt Chinese babies began to dwindle in the years that we waited. Remarkably, China had, at the time, the best reputation worldwide for adoption access to healthy, female babies. Africa was difficult to access. The word amongst adoptive parents was that the adoption industry in Russia and Eastern Europe was riddled with corruption and other countries had a smaller adoption infrastructure, exorbitant fees, or limited access to healthy newborn infants. China had been our best bet.

But we had gambled and lost. Months went by, then years, and still no word as to when we might travel to China, despite some sporadic angry protestations from the families involved.

Of course, the agency could have no hand in the dramatic change in China's efforts to control its female population by allowing foreigners to adopt the female newborns. To put it crudely, I believe the supply of newborns was drying up just at the moment we and thousands of other Westerners were yearning for an adopted child from China. It could have been the improving economy in China that made Chinese parents less desperate and forced to give up their baby girls. It could have been the Chinese government's belated discovery that they were effectively eliminating the possibility of young Chinese males finding marriage partners.

I think the agency was astute enough to see the change slowly evolving in their relations with the Chinese government and it was dishonest of it to continue to solicit and sign up parents and put them on this horrendous years-long waiting list after the families had each made an expenditure of several thousand dollars they would never get back in the event they were unable to go to China or could not withstand the delay of waiting for a child. Some families in our group went to Africa to adopt, while we waited for word from the agency. Three days before Family Day in 2013, we were now faced with the dilemma of how to proceed. We had been waiting several years and now had only a few days to decide.

I did not think I could face the challenges of being a new mother on the wrong side of fifty and deal with the issue of Frankie's transition as well. My nerves and emotional resources had been stretched beyond anything I could have imagined. Even though I was somewhat willing to try and proceed with the adoption in China, I knew Rob was morally and emotionally exhausted as well. All the goodwill and hope that we had experienced in wanting to adopt had disappeared. Only Frankie was enthusiastic and positive about proceeding but then, this would not be his child to raise nor his situation to manage. It was ours and ours alone.

I had another unspoken fear; with the gravity of Frankie's emotional and physical changes, would he be able to care for this much younger child in the event of our illness or early death? There would be a fifteen-year age difference. Chillingly, we realized that we, as parents, would be seventy when this child graduated from high school. Was that a fair burden to place on Frankie in light of his struggles to come out and transition?

Frankie was pro-adoption. I was on the fence. Rob, regretfully, could not see proceeding. Why was Frankie so positive regarding the adoption of a little sister? There seemed to be no competitiveness or jealousy. I know he desperately wanted siblings and had begged for them for years. Even while I was going through fertility treatments and trying to conceive with my sister's eggs, I did not speak to Frankie about the procedures. I didn't want to burden Frankie with our sorrows and difficulties. I didn't want to see Frankie suffer through the numerous disappointments. But now I wonder, did he have an ulterior motive? Did he think, unconsciously, this was an opportunity for his mother to have the little girl she had always hoped for? Would that relieve some of the pressure on him? Would I one day find a use for the unfinished dollhouse?

In the end, with extreme regret, I contacted the agency by email and told them we could not proceed. There was much I wanted to say, but could not. I could not communicate how much bitterness, anger, and regret I had come to feel over this futile and heartbreaking episode in our lives.

Perversely, I also felt an odd sense of relief that I had not succumbed to the desire to furnish the baby's new room that we had situated beside Frankie's bedroom or buy the baby clothes or items for her care. I had begged off the numerous bags of baby clothes and toys my sister-in-law had generously offered to give me. My European peasant's superstition, or a premonition of what was to come, perhaps, had urged me to wait, to see if it would transpire. To paint the baby's room in anticipation, to buy the pretty clothes I often gazed at with longing, to accept the wonderful gifts of toys and accessories, was tempting fate. And me and fate weren't on good terms.

I had allowed myself only one purchase for the prospective baby whom, we decided, we would name Isabella — a small denim jacket with embroidered lapels, pretty and feminine, and the smallest size I had ever seen. I had stashed it away in my clothes closet in our bedroom, out of sight, where I would not be tempted to buy any more articles of clothing.

It remains there still, behind the heart-shaped gift boxes, the wrapping paper and the ribbons, and the small baby gifts that I periodically purchase and save for the next baby to be born into our large circle of family and friends. I'd also had a dim hope in the back of my mind that the new baby would one day also come to love the unfinished dollhouse.

# Purge

❖

I HAD TO THINK ABOUT giving away Frankie's cradle, one that I have clung to since his birth.

Our neighbourhood holds an annual garage sale that extends over several streets. Our participation has been sporadic over the almost seventeen years we have lived in our much-loved home. We don't make much at the sales, but it's a good way to clear the house of unwanted stuff that has accumulated. The longer we are together, the more we accumulate.

A few years ago we decided to sell a lot of Frankie's larger baby stuff: a portable playpen, a swinging chair, the car seat, some bits and pieces from Frankie's babyhood. I had mixed feelings about this. I had been holding on to the stuff for the second baby that never came and then the adoption that never happened.

The morning started badly the day of the sale. Frankie had been ill during the night. I got up to lie beside him at four-thirty a.m. Four-thirty is a bad time for me. It usually means I won't return to sleep. Frankie managed to fall asleep, but I did not. Unfortunately, Rob didn't wake up feeling that great either.

I had two unwell family members on my hands and a whole bunch of stuff that I had to set up on a table on the lawn in front of our house. Books, toys, knickknacks, two pairs of skates, two bikes, many child-sized hockey sticks, a stereo. Rob dragged himself outside to help me with the big stuff, then collapsed on the couch, creeping out periodically into the sun like a resurrected vampire, shielding his eyes with sunglasses and looking a tad green.

As I sat there in the June morning sun, which was pleasant and warm, I realized I was immensely annoyed and saddened. I was alone for most of the sale and I was furious. But why? It was the baby stuff. I didn't want to give it away, but what was the point of holding on to the big articles? Some precious toys and clothes and books I kept. But for whom? For Frankie's babies, if they came? When? Fifteen years from then? If I was lucky?

Every six months, Rob and I have an enormous argument about a wooden cradle my sister got for me when Frankie was born. This item didn't make it into the garage sale. I refused to put it out. I thought it was pretty steady in its structure, though you could not place an infant in it with today's safety standards. But I kept it in Frankie's room. I piled it high with the dozens of stuffies Frankie had received as gifts when he was a baby — many, many dozens. It gave me such pleasure just to look at it. It gave his room a homey feel.

Rob wanted to get rid of it. He explained that we had no need for it. It was not particularly well constructed, it was difficult to move around because it was fragile, and it invariably fell apart in our hands whenever I moved it to get to something else. All true. But if I gave it up, wasn't I saying that's it? Acknowledging that we would never have another child, biological or otherwise? *Aye, there's the rub.* I clung to the damn thing and refused to give it away. And I fought with Rob each time he said we should get rid of it. He was done with this issue, done. I didn't blame him — it had been years of frustration and sorrow and not a small amount of bitterness.

The cradle was full of unanswered questions. Shouldn't we have? Why didn't we? Why couldn't we? Why didn't you? The cradle became the symbol of our infertility for me — *my* infertility. I was angry at myself and him and the whole damn world for the way things had turned out. I felt guilty because I knew I was being selfish. I had a child. Many women did not have one and desperately wanted one. And Frankie was a beautiful, wondrous child.

Still.

I was a greedy thing. I did not feel that I was done with motherhood and small babies. "Baby lust," they call it. So I pined. And I waited. And waited.

THE MORNING OF GARAGE-SALE day had a semi-happy ending. My sister called and said she might be in need of some of the baby stuff. She was a foster parent for the Children's Aid Society and might get a baby to care for over the summer. Could she have the portable playpen, car seat, swinging chair? *Could she?* I was so relieved that I didn't have to sell these items to a stranger that I would have carried that stuff on my own back to get them to her in Hamilton. And the cradle? Eventually she would take that back, too, for her partner's son's new baby.

# My Kingdom of Three

✦

IT WAS A VERY LONG time before I spoke to family and friends about Frankie's transition after he came out. There were so many conflicting feelings in me — confusion, fear, anxiety, an intense need to protect Frankie, anger, embarrassment, a lack of understanding as to what was happening, a fierce love. I couldn't begin to sort out my feelings. We didn't tell people immediately. But eventually the inner circle knew. The outer circle did not.

Our inner circle included my mother, our siblings on both sides, very close friends, Frankie's close friends and school-mates and, by necessity, Frankie's school. Our outer circle included people at our respective workplaces, the extended family of cousins, aunts, and uncles on both sides of the family, neighbours, and random strangers who might innocently ask, "Do you have any kids?" to which I would answer "yes." They would ask, "How many?" I would say, "One." "A son or daughter?" *Where do I start*, I often thought, uncomfortably.

Once a colleague at a social event asked if I had a daughter.

I had attended the lunch with some other work friends. I hesitated and looked up at someone I was close to who knew our situation. The inquirer looked at me with wonder and said, "It's *not* that complicated!" *Sister, if you only knew*, I thought. At times, this kind of situation created a form of schizophrenia in my mind regarding pronouns. I used *she, her*, and *daughter* at work, with neighbours or with strangers. Within the family, I used *he, him*, and *son*. But I would slip up and this risked Frankie's wrath and frustration. I had great anxiety about messing up the pronouns. I know at work I slipped once or twice and it must have seemed very odd that I appeared not to know the gender of my own child, although no one commented on it.

My hesitation in telling people was a tremendous source of irritation for Frankie. "Just *tell* them," he said. "*I'm a boy now.* I want to be referred to *as a boy.*" He had told all his friends and they, without exception, appeared to follow his lead quite effortlessly. I was shocked, yet comforted, by the ease with which he made the transition within his own circle of friends and at school. This gave me a great deal of hope for the future — the receptiveness and lack of drama in Frankie's community of friends was heartening. Say what you will about millennials, most are more open and less conflicted on issues of sexuality and gender. There was only one occasion that Frankie told me about where someone referred to Frankie as an *it* within his earshot at an otherwise friendly gathering. Beware, young man, lest I meet you on the street one dark night.

When a male friend of Frankie's from middle school with

a dodgy reputation as a player tried to contact Frankie online through social media, I warned Frankie about this guy's possible intentions. Frankie just blithely responded, "Don't worry, he knows I'm a boy now."

I broke the ice within my circle by telling them that Frankie had a girlfriend. I was able to gauge their response to the news that Frankie was dating a girl. They seemed surprised, but did not respond negatively, for the most part. I tried to avoid saying Frankie was gay as this was not the truth, nor was it the way he described himself; but the real situation was too raw, too complicated, to be explained initially.

"I don't consider myself gay," he had said before he came out as trans; he obviously was unprepared then to tell me what was really happening. This caused a great deal of confusion on my part. You're a girl and you like girls, right? I think that means you're gay. Why are you saying you are not?

Most of my friends were nonplussed, but some I knew were uneasy. That wasn't my problem, I reasoned, so I tried to ignore the feeling that they disapproved. If they seemed relatively comfortable with what I had told them, eventually I would tell them it was far more complex than being gay, because that's not truly what Frankie was.

Eventually, one by one, I explained that Frankie was trans. Sometimes I did this in person, but frequently I did it by email if I was addressing someone I did not see regularly. I would explain Frankie's health issues and treatment and then what was at the root of this illness and suffering for the last five years. I would emphasize that his unburdening had immediately had a salutary effect on him — in terms of his physical and mental health, his school attendance, his grades, social activities, and his engagement with the outside world.

It was interesting to see how people reacted in person. My circle, which included very close friends and one or two workmates whom I knew I could trust, often looked like I had dropped a bomb on them; they were stricken, shocked. They were almost all parents of children of varying ages — some much younger than Frankie. They couldn't seem to fathom it initially. Some were literally, momentarily, speechless. But they soon recovered and were discreet in their responses, supportive, sympathetic, kind. They could see what it had cost me to tell them and they weren't going to make me more uncomfortable than I already was. But sometimes the questions — and of course there were questions — were intrusive and a bit obtuse.

What kind of surgery would Frankie have? they might ask. How far will he go with the transition? What has he done so far? What is his real birth name? How did *your* family, the *Italian* side react? Very nicely, thank you. He has a *girlfriend*? Does the girlfriend's family accept him? Are you uncomfortable with his appearance? Are you uncomfortable being with him in public?

Then there was the group of people who appeared to be not-so-committed to the transition or us. The one-obligatory-brunch-or-dinner-and-that's-it crowd. We had a surge of invitations to have a meal. These people were polite; they never referred to the transition during the meal, and would reluctantly engage in the subject only if we brought it up. They avoided the pesky issue of pronouns — neither using he nor she. Gingerly, they broached Frankie's future plans and his current state of health. They were not hostile, but profoundly uncomfortable in the situation. And then we never really heard from them again. They were not unfriendly, they just weren't around. I imagined them closing the door after we left and then, after heaving a sigh of relief, saying to themselves, "Well, good luck with *that*."

There were some family members who stopped talking to us. A very small group. Or there were the family members and acquaintances who never spoke of Frankie again, as if he had died and it was impolite or unseemly to mention his name, as if we would be overwhelmed with grief if they mentioned his name. We don't see those people anymore.

We, my kingdom of three — Frankie, Rob, and me — formed an emotional fortress around ourselves. I have a theory that people always view you in connection to the most traumatic thing that has ever happened to you — widowed, stricken with cancer, an ill child, a bad divorce. These circumstances always colour how you are perceived. But as long as Frankie was well and thriving, nothing could ever hurt me again. I would never again come almost to the breaking point as I had when he was ill. Nothing could hurt me like that. I told myself I was unbreakable.

IN MAY OF 2014, I attended a conference of writers and poets in Montreal and decided to read a portion of my work related to Frankie's transition, finally outing myself to my writing colleagues, some of whom I had known for decades. The response was warm and receptive, although I was unnerved by what appeared to be two very highly strung ladies who pounced on me after the reading with questions. This is not, I have observed, an unusual position to be in when one reads controversial material in public.

The first one advanced boldly. She was older, harried, and seemed to have something urgent to ask me. She did. As she approached, she blurted out, without introducing herself, "Is she a boy yet?"

"I'm sorry?" I responded politely.

"Frankie … is she a boy yet?"

"Frankie is transitioning … she's in the process of … She …"

She scooted away as violently and abruptly as she had approached me. I had not really finished my answer properly.

The second lady approached; again, with no introduction, she just bravely plunged right into it. Grey-haired, vaguely hippie-ish, with a frizzy afro, a voluminous summer dress, and big earrings, a little agitated. Was it the topic that incensed her or was she just a little off? I wondered. She seemed anxious.

"Why can't she just wait until she's eighteen to do all this stuff?" she asked in an irritable tone that she utterly failed to conceal. By "stuff" I assumed she meant the name change, the pronoun change, the clothing and piercings, the prospective testosterone injections, and the top surgery.

"It's … complicated," I said. I wasn't about to get into this with a stranger.

"Well, I don't understand why she just can't wait." She went on, but I can't recall the rest. Eventually, she too flounced away.

I am amazed how people feel they can advise you on the most intimate details of your family situation. A few friends who surrounded me after the reading gave me uncomfortable looks of sympathy. *But, really* I thought, *it doesn't matter what people say.* Sometimes I find in these situations I can be surprisingly thick-skinned. *Don't make me choose between my child and you*, I often thought during these difficult periods.

# The Night is My Nemesis

✦

THE NIGHT IS MY NEMESIS. Neither Frankie nor I seemed to be able to conquer it. This problem arose in my university days and I have yet to surmount it. We both had the sort of personalities that go over the same negative or worrisome thoughts obsessively before we go to sleep. These circle around us — like troublesome, menacing birds on a merciless loop without end — getting progressively more threatening as the night goes on. It sometimes took us hours to go to sleep. Frankie used to come to me for comfort, crawl into bed with me and Rob for a short time, until he was less tense or anxious. Now he had begun to try to tackle it on his own, sometimes successfully, sometimes not. I knew it was an illusion, but I always felt safer when Frankie was wedged between me and Rob in the bed at night — as if I could protect him from anything when we are together.

If he was out at night, alone, I could not rest until he was home and safe. Rob repeatedly asked me to leave Frankie alone, not to text him, not to call him, not to make him afraid of the city, of the night, of all the night might hold for him.

Many nights, I lay awake interminably waiting for sleep. Sometimes I played the radio a bit too loudly to shake myself from my thoughts. This risked waking Rob who, most nights, was blissfully unaware of my nightly torment. I changed beds for relief — opting to move to the middle bedroom on the second floor, which was cooler and darker and had the added benefit of being closer to Frankie in case he needed me. Occasionally I read something light and pointless when I couldn't concentrate fully. Sometimes I resorted to sleeping pills — anything to alleviate the anxiety.

My thoughts always went to the same place. Would Frankie successfully transition? What would become of my child as an adult? What would people think of him, of me, of my family? Would they blame me? Did I do something wrong somehow? Had I wronged Frankie in not moving quickly enough? Did I have the moral courage to proceed?

Often, I felt I did not have the courage required to support Frankie. I marvelled at his determination and guts. This child, my son, could be, if required, fierce and fearless — approaching hostile strangers and admonishing them for their unfriendly appraisal of his appearance, challenging people who annoyed his then girlfriend, urging me to be transparent and brave with family and friends, and continuing to make the physical changes that the transition requires, despite the confusion and doubt of those around him.

If I possibly could bequeath one thing to my child it would be peace of mind. I certainly wished I had it.

SINCE THE BEGINNING OF THE transition, I dreamt about Frankie constantly. Before the transition I hardly ever dreamed of Frankie or Rob. The dreams were utterly banal, but always had a strange twist. No need to consult Dr. Freud on these; the meaning is pretty clear.

Dream #1
Rob and I are walking down the street and find a little boy. He is alone, abandoned. He appears to be from Central America. He is olive-skinned and looks part Hispanic, part aboriginal. He is one angry little boy, although it is not clear why. We take him home and love him and he changes. He is happy!

Dream #2
It's *Take your kid to work* day. Frankie is very little, as she was at five or six. I wake her up gently and take her to work. When we get there, there is an enormous bed. I put her down to sleep and tell her I will wake her shortly, once work starts.

Dream #3
Frankie and I fly away, literally *fly away*, through the sky and across an ocean. The exterior of a house looks like a large, gorgeous stone cottage that sits on the ocean but the inside is a beautiful apartment filled with books and beautiful objects and wonderful food and music. The atmosphere is welcoming and convivial. I don't recognize anyone, but they are clearly family and friends. Outside is a storm that batters the house, inside all is calm and beautiful.

# Buon Giorno Principessa

❖

WHEN FRANKIE WAS BORN, I bought her a pretty white dish and a small cup from a sweet little store on Queen West that carried these cute, eclectic household items. They had a series with the greeting *Buon Giorno Principessa* (Good Morning Princess) emblazoned on it —a reference to the daily greeting Roberto Benigni's character makes to a woman he is wooing in the film *Life is Beautiful*. It gave me so much pleasure to use it for Frankie's meals when she was a baby. The endearing pink daisy graphic on the dish, the familiar phrase in a quirky font, the sweetness of the salutation. She *was* my princess with her luscious chocolate curls and rosebud mouth. Even though I don't think we especially spoiled Frankie, it's difficult with only one child not to do so. I liked the dish and cup so much I bought similar ones for all three of my nieces.

Now my princess was becoming a prince as he embarked on testosterone therapy that would change his look quite a bit. Frankie had been a good boy, doing all that was requested by the Gender Identity Clinic that authorized his hormone therapy. He attended his therapy sessions, and he went to school devotedly for most of the year, despite having some bad days and periods. Frankie had excellent grades in the final year of high school and was accepted to the university of his choice. He began to re-engage with family and friends. He worked on his art and dabbled again with his music.

The head of the Gender Identity Clinic gave him a good progress review and Frankie was permitted to see an endo-crinologist, who authorized the testosterone injections by the family doctor. Masculinizing hormone therapy has vital psychological benefits for a trans man (born female, transitioned/ing to male). Understandably, it eases gender dysphoria and helps trans men feel better about their bodies. It can make them less anxious, less depressed, calmer. All good things.

However, there are changes ahead. Some of these are irreversible. A deeper voice, increased muscle mass, oilier skin, and possibly male pattern baldness. There would be facial hair, quantity unknown. The long-term effects of testos-terone on fertility are not fully documented or understood. Frankie may become permanently sterile, even if he stopped taking testosterone at some point. There are serious possible side effects: increase of bad cholesterol, greater fat depos-its, heightened blood pressure, possible weight gain, mood changes, and increased aggression.

The potential of possible sterility became the source of many heated arguments between Frankie and me. Usually I lost them; I would withdraw in defeat and sometimes tears of frustration. In the end, Frankie thought that feeling more secure in his identity outweighed the possibility of sterility. I was unsure, but it wasn't my life. Frankie would soon be eighteen and it would be out of my hands. I could not control his life or how he chose to live it.

I RECENTLY HAD A DISCUSSION with a woman, another mother of an only child. We did not have a particularly close relationship — more casual acquaintances than friends. I had read passages of a blog I was writing on the transition to an audience and she had sent me a touching note about her own daughter coming out gay. That was a shock for me. This friend is usually very open about her life as a woman and mother, and as an artist and a poet. She had never mentioned this in public. One of her sadnesses surrounding her daughter's sexuality was the fact that she would not be a grandmother. Of course, it was not impossible, but it seems that for now, her daughter has indicated it likely would not happen. And the mother longs for it.

Is it ironic that someone like me, who at one time did not wish to marry or have children, now longs for the future grandchildren that I will likely never have? Ironic or a bit pathetic? And this is not strictly true as Frankie, who loves babies, is adamant that he will have children, adopted or otherwise. Is it silly that I want biological grandchildren — blood of my blood — the children of my child named for a Sicilian bandit and a Roman empress?

Some might use another word for my behaviour.

IT WAS ONE OF THOSE scenarios where a parent thinks, *That's what my child was trying to tell me! Why didn't I see that? It's so obvious now* ...

Any Canadian with a teenager will be familiar with *Degrassi*, the teen drama, and perhaps may also be aware of the character of the transgender teen Adam Torres played by the actress Jordan Todosey. I have to admit that the figure of Adam was a mystery to me before I had any awareness of Frankie's inner life and struggles as a transgender teen. Frankie would fall into a snit if I referred to Adam as she when I periodically caught a glimpse of him on the series. My thinking was — and I *thought* logically — but she's biologically a girl, why are we pretending that she is not?

The character of Adam was very distinctly pretty-looking in appearance, despite the boy's haircut and clothing. The voice was light and high, the character looked like a girl playing at being a boy. That might have been a treasonous thought, given my circumstances, but it's what I thought. It enraged Frankie when I futilely pursued my argument with him. His position was simple: "If the character of Adam wants to be referred to as a male, then that's what we should do. It doesn't matter what you think you see, *he* sees himself as a male."

Agreed. I see that now — but then I was mystified by Frankie's vehemence on the issue.

LATER, I LEARNED, READING A section of something Frankie had written for CAMH, that watching the Adam character on the show had triggered something in him. He watched with wonder as the Adam character bound his breasts on one of the shows. Frankie then snuck into the medicine cabinet and took out some ACE bandages and tried to do the same to himself only to break down in tears as it was unsuccessful. He had to suppress the sound of his crying as his dad was in the next room.

It uncomfortably reminded me of a similar discussion I had with a work colleague many years before. He was friends with a trans woman (transitioning from male to female). This person was born male, *presented* as male, but preferred to be referred to as she and her. I was puzzled and irritated by this, partly because this same person became furious if someone referred to her as male. *But how are we to know?* I blithely argued, *if he presents as male?* My friend mildly interjected that that was what his friend wanted, so he was honouring that. I was adamant in my position.

Of course, realistically, you can't know, unless you are told by the person you are interacting with how they would prefer to be seen and referred to. But this is where we have to step up as parents and people who have trans people in our lives. I am reminded repeatedly that Frankie prefers male pronouns — at first it was a polite request, then it became more an irritated demand. It was a hard lesson for me, honouring that request. I stumbled, quite often, usually catching myself but not always. I'd say the majority of the conflicts I had with Frankie revolved around the use of the correct pronouns.

But Frankie's distress also reminded me of a period in my life as a young teenager where I had longish, shaggy hair, wore boyish jeans or cords most of the time, and was repeatedly mistaken for a boy. The constant confusion, too, would enrage me as a young girl struggling to define my look as a female.

Clearly, we need to tread carefully, unlike me in the situations described above. It might be confusing or upsetting or disturbing when the personal pronoun you wish to use appears at odds with the visual representation, but trans people deserve that minimum level of respect. I think I've learned that the hard way.

ONCE ROB HAD RECONCILED HIMSELF to the fact that Frankie was going to transition from female to male, he developed a strangely nurturing attitude towards how Frankie should behave as a newly minted young man. He mentioned specifically that he was disappointed that Frankie did not escort his new girlfriend home on late nights. Frankie's girlfriend lived east of us, perhaps ten minutes by car, but the kids travelled by public transit as neither had their driver's licences. However, I was thinking *Whoa, wait a minute*, boy or girl, Frankie is still only about five-foot-four and less than one hundred-twenty pounds and you want him to travel late at night, by himself, after he drops off his girlfriend?

Why do we have to go down this road? I silently pleaded. My anxiety level was already sky high regarding Frankie's physical safety when he was not with me because I was afraid how people would react to him and the ambiguity of his gender. Frankie going out at night was often agonising for me, as I kept imagining the worst. If he was late, the anxiety started to mount and then I would text him, trying to sound as casual as possible: *Are you close? Do you need a ride? Are you on your own? Who is with you? What time will you be home?*

Rob would keep giving me warning looks and utter quiet asides while I texted:

"Don't freak him out."

"You are communicating your anxiety."

"Don't make him afraid of the city."

"I don't want him to be afraid."

One night, Frankie called from the streetcar stop near our house. He was clearly upset. He was on his way home by transit, he said. He was shaking and in tears when he reached our porch late that night. Unusually, three disturbing things had happened all in one night. Frankie had been invited to a Chinese restaurant where some school friends were meeting. Some of Frankie's schoolmates — not Frankie's close friends — were sitting at an adjacent table and, he suspected, were giggling and talking about him. This unnerved him as he was accustomed to general acceptance and respect from his school and his schoolmates.

When Frankie and a female friend left the restaurant and got on the subway they attracted attention from some older adults sitting across from them who appeared curious about their appearance and started to parse Frankie's appearance. Frankie suspected they were gay. Frankie had his headphones on and was gazing upwards, but could clearly hear what they were saying. One stranger, staring the kids down, explained to his companion that Frankie was trans and that his companion was probably his girlfriend, which she was not. This was hurtful and rude, but not overwhelmingly so for Frankie.

When Frankie changed connections on the subway line, he had the misfortune of encountering a group of boys on the platform and the way one of them was looking at Frankie rattled him. He felt, for the first time, physically threatened because of his gender. Not that something bad had happened, but that something bad *could* happen. The boy was evidently trying to intimidate Frankie. What could my kid do in response? He'd never been in a physical altercation. He'd never been struck or struck anyone in his life.

After Frankie came home and told us, I too was shaken by his experience. Who, I wondered, will make sure my child is safe in the world when we are gone?

# Ash Wednesday

✦

PART OF THE REASON I was uncomfortable talking to people about Frankie's transition, even close friends and family, was the usual platitudes we received about what great parents we were, about how wonderful we were. This made me very uneasy. They really didn't seem to understand the situation.

Your kid comes to you and says, "I know you think I'm an apple but I'm an orange. I may look like an apple but, inside, I feel that I'm an orange." Who am I to say, "No, you're not. You're like me, I don't care what you think. You're an apple." Who am I, who are you, to say to Frankie, "You are wrong and you should conform with what society thinks they see in you"? I can't think of a single parent I know who would turn her back on her child in this situation. I'm not naive, I know it happens, but I think most people would do the right thing, as painful as it might be for them. We don't want to play the heroes in this scenario because we are not. Frankie is.

My child feels that he has to go down a certain path. It may make me uneasy and uncomfortable, afraid, confused, angry at times, but how can I not assist him down that path? And if my child is now legally an adult and wants to do this, how would I be able to stop him without irreparable emotional damage to our relationship?

It was still with enormous trepidation that I began to approach informing Frankie's school, our families, and our friends with the truth about Frankie's transition. As Frankie neared his seventeenth birthday in November of 2013, he was adamant that we begin to tell people explicitly what was going on.

The school was relatively easy. Here, Frankie took the lead with a newfound confidence, approaching the guidance counsellor at school, who informed the vice principal. The VP called me to confirm that this was all done with my knowledge. That was, thankfully, a painless conversation conducted with tact and kindness. The truth is that once we came to accept his situation, Frankie grew immeasurably stronger and more confident emotionally and physically. He missed less school; he started to engage with friends and family again. The physical ailments disappeared, for the most part. He had his blue days, his off days, but now they numbered two or three a month rather than two or three a week. He was empowered by our acceptance, by our love.

ROB TOLD HIS SIBLINGS AND I told my mine. The idea of speaking to the immediate side of my family, which is more conservative and Catholic than Rob's side of the family, made me nervous. What was I afraid of? I was afraid that I would have to choose between my extended family and my child. I knew who would win that contest. I did not want to lose my family. I was afraid they would blame me as the mother. I was afraid of my mother's reaction. I was afraid that they would not act normally with Frankie. I was afraid that I — and Rob and Frankie — would be judged and condemned.

I was very nervous when I spoke to my brother Charlie on the telephone, but he was thoughtful and very gentle with me. He was not entirely surprised and he reassured me that the whole family loved Frankie and would support him no matter what. He also offered to take a bullet for me in speaking to my mother, which was the conversation that had me most worried. She was troubled by this new information — she was almost eighty then — but accepting and loving.

A few days later, we celebrated Frankie's seventeenth birthday at our home in an atmosphere of love and support. If our families were anxious or upset, they hid it well and treated Frankie with great kindness. Slowly over the Christmas holidays I began to tell people that I was close to. Unanimously they were kind, supportive, loving, and non-judgmental. I felt I had been relieved of an enormous burden.

BUT I DID HAVE MY days of doubt and despair. I found myself resorting to old ways of consolation that have been engrained in me since birth. I thought I had moved beyond this sort of consolation. For several years, I had been attending mass on Ash Wednesday at the Catholic church on the university campus where I work. It marks the beginning of Lent for Christians, the season of penitential preparation for the feast of Easter. Lapsed — or recovering — Catholic that I was, I still found a quiet pleasure in this time. I did not go to mass during the year. I usually went alone on Ash Wednesday and told no one. It's like a secret vice that I won't admit to as a committed agnostic. I sometimes wiped the ashes from my forehead after church and usually didn't mention it to Rob, who, as a non-Catholic, was a bit perturbed by the ritual.

I did not consider myself a religious person, but in times of great stress I found myself turning to the actual physical beauty of the church for comfort. I was not guided by the precepts of the Catholic church, but I found solace in the actual bricks and mortar of the physical space where I once worshipped as a child and teenager.

THE CURRENT POPE, FRANCIS, AUGURS better things to come for all human beings and how we treat them, especially the poor. I like him very much, but I can't ignore the Church's continuing position on the role of women in the Church, the right for women to control their bodies, and the right to love and marry whomever you want. The Church's views stand against most of my moral principles. This is why I left.

But I admit that I am seduced by the beauty of a Catholic church. No other place of worship inspires me in the same manner. The church on campus is sadly bereft of vivid imagery, feeling more Protestant than Catholic, unlike the church where my parents, and many of my relations, married. All Souls Church in Hamilton was the scene of my debut as a flower girl where I petulantly declared that I would never marry again after a trying day of being complimented and feted at my aunt's wedding. At All Souls, five angels dressed in gowns of blue and gold and pink flank the large crucifix above the altar. The dome of the church is a multi-hued vision of heaven with the Virgin Mary and her Child at its centre and all the angels seeming to turn to, and defer to, Mary rather than a more ominous looking God poised directly above her. The Victorian cherubs at Mary's left and right sides remind me of the picture of the two angels I placed in Frankie's crib when she was a toddler. Once she could speak, she begged me to remove them. They terrified her. I thought it a pretty addition to her lovely bedroom and crib, but she disliked them intensely.

The architecture of this church, its stained-glass windows, its statues and paintings, the vibrant garments of the priests, its solitude and peacefulness are soothing to me. The blandly placid faces of the statues of the saints and the Virgin Mary console me. The lighting and burning of the candles enshrouded in blood-red glass is reassuring. The sense of hope it engenders when you light a candle for a person you care for. The smell of the incense. The progression of the Stations of the Cross along the walls of the church. It is an intense sensory experience that is difficult to ignore or forget.

Ash Wednesday holds an enormous appeal for me. A mysterious process and ceremony, it confounds and alarms the outsider. What does the cross of ashes spread on the forehead symbolize? The pouring of ashes on one's body is an ancient Christian ritual, an "outer manifestation of inner repentance or mourning."

During the service, I find myself doing precisely that: mourning, grieving, repenting, trying to think what I might have done to influence how our lives have evolved. But as I educate myself about our child's situation, I realize these are futile and foolish thoughts. Frankie did not choose this path. I did not choose to treat him in a certain way and thus he developed into a trans person. However, he did choose, bravely, to try and live an open and honest life. He is trying to live a life that is true to his inner desires and feelings. That takes an enormous amount of guts. My son has more courage in him than most people I know.

ON THAT ASH WEDNESDAY I mourned my wasted emotions and anguish, my unspoken, guilt-ridden desire for a different outcome. I repented my misdirected anger and frustration. I asked for patience, forbearance, and an open heart. I asked for peace. I wanted it so desperately. I wanted to be soothed, to have the anger and frustration drain out of me. I wanted to be patient, to be kind, to let go of the fantasy of the life I thought I would lead when I married and when I gave birth to my only child. Because that fantasy, if I clung to it, if I insisted that my child adhere to it, despite his reservations and sorrows, would destroy my child.

*Mea culpa, mea culpa, mea culpa.*

# Untagged

✦

THE START OF MOTHER'S DAY was lovely. Rob and I were cooking two meals to be shared — one at my sister's home and one at my in-laws' home. We always have two family gatherings on Mother's Day — one for each side of the family. When I was pregnant with Frankie in the spring of 1996, I started gathering the moms in our extended families together for a meal and an exchange of small gifts. It's a lovely gathering of three generations: my mom, sister, various sisters-in-law, and, the mother of my sisters — and brothers-in-law.

As things were bubbling along in the kitchen, I hopped on social media to post a picture of Frankie and me to celebrate Mother's Day. It was my absolute favourite photograph — it's from the summer of 1997, when Frankie was about six or seven months old. We are sitting in the living room of the old house where Frankie was first raised and lived until she was three. On the bookcase behind us is a row of books by my favourite female writers. I am looking away from the camera and smiling. Frankie looks a bit pensive: the round little face, sad eyes, and downturned mouth are so sweet. She is wearing a little grey dress with a black-and-white pattern and white T-shirt underneath. Her little arms are plump with good health. Her beautiful honey-coloured arms are stretched around my torso and I am cupping her in my arms. I am holding someone precious.

I clicked on Tag Photo and put my name in and then I clicked on Frankie's face to add his name and I got this message: *Cannot tag photo. This person or page cannot be tagged because they have previously removed their tag from this photo.*

What? I was so agitated and surprised, I burst into tears. Why would Frankie do that — especially when I had said repeatedly that it was my favourite photo? While in the midst of cooking, Rob rushed over to see what was wrong with me. He was sympathetic, but more conciliatory. He thought perhaps Frankie wanted to banish all photos of himself on Facebook where he was explicitly seen as female. But why did my memories have to be destroyed as well? I thought, somewhat peevishly.

Frankie's name had been changed legally, his physical look and clothing had changed. Frankie even mildly objected to old photos on display in the house of him as a young person. But these were our memories too and they were not deeply unpleasant for us. Quite the contrary. I dug in my heels. Why did my happy past have to be obliterated? Why couldn't I retain that?

I spent the next hour or so in utter misery. Rob told me, reasonably, to speak to Frankie. I said no, I was too emotional. Frankie, asleep, was still blissfully unaware of my disappointment. I didn't want to get into it and spoil the day.

An hour later, Frankie came down. He had a Mother's Day gift behind his back as he approached me. He had a lovely smile. Uncannily, Frankie is the single person most attuned to my emotions. He immediately knows when I am angry or agitated or sad. His face dropped and he asked me what was wrong.

"Nothing," I said. I couldn't explain, I was so distressed.

"Please tell me," Frankie said.

He persisted.

I explained.

"Mom," he said in genuine wonder. "I don't even remember doing that!"

I had a very snippy response. "Well, you are the only one who could have done it. That's how Facebook works."

As I calmed down a bit and we talked about it, we came to the conclusion that Frankie's untagging of photos had possibly happened a few years ago when he was having trouble with Julia's bothersome, then openly homophobic mother who was trying to contact Frankie on social media. We didn't want her to see anything to do with Frankie or the family so I had asked Frankie to untag himself. This was likely it.

Still, why was I so rattled by this innocuous act? Because I love my role as a mother and I specifically enjoyed being the mother of a daughter. I cherished it. The thought of changing that role saddens me.

But, put very simply, it is not about what I want. Not anymore. Untagged or not, it's a new world now.

# She's the Man

✦

FRANKIE HAS TAKEN TO LEARNING how to shave, as he has experienced more hair growth with the testosterone injections. Every few weeks he goes to the family doctor with a prescription and gets an injection that will increase facial and body hair growth, deepen his voice, and stop the menstrual flow that would have come monthly. His face and body will be leaner.

These are the injections he literally begged for when he came out at sixteen. He was distraught. "I need something to change. I need something to change," he implored on the verge of tears, rocking back and forth, agitated in a manner I had not seen before. He frightened me terribly. I thought he might be on the cusp of some desperate act, that he might harm himself. I think what he was saying was that this state of ambiguity, looking like a girl, feeling like a boy, was too disturbing and he needed to alter the physical to match the emotional.

Rob teaches Frankie to shave discreetly, as it initially unnerved me. Rob is instructing Frankie; Frankie is anxiously watching for new growth every time he shaves. They have both learned that anything that has to do with the physical transformation is upsetting to me and they try and be sensitive about it. One time I roughly told both of them that I did not want to know about this part of the transition. I was not opposing it, but I didn't want to witness it either. I know this was disappointing to Frankie, but there was only so much I could experience or witness without being an impediment to his happiness because I was anxious or melancholy about the changes.

When Frankie started going for hormone replacement therapy, he selected his dad as the person who would help him learn how to eventually do the injections himself. That was the ultimate goal. There were two reasons behind this favouring of Rob: First, I can't stand seeing Frankie in pain. Remember my squeamishness when they were drawing blood from Frankie's heel to test the bilirubin level when he was a preemie? That hasn't changed one bit. Secondly, thinking of the long-term implications of how Frankie's look will change is still distressing.

When we first began to have our tentative tear-filled discussions about the transition, Frankie asked me why I was uncomfortable with the physical change. I love the way he looks, he is beautiful to me, I said. Most, if not all, mothers feel this way. I told him, truthfully, I found the disparity between how a trans person *desired* to look and how she or he *did* look very unsettling sometimes, and very saddening. I hated the snickering manner in which trans people are discussed in the popular media. But I have to acknowledge that my attitude has not been much better.

Frankie was on a mission to prove to me that it did not

have to be so. He kept bringing me photos of trans men — that particular list of men he showed me eludes me now but I have since amassed my own mental list of very attractive and successful transitions: Balian Buschbaum, a former German pole vaulter; Loren Rex Cameron, an American photographer, author, and transsexual activist; Ian Harvie, a standup comedian; Ryan Sallans, LGBTQ rights advocate; Rocco Kayiatos (known as Katastrophe), an American hip-hop rapper and producer; and Andreas Krieger, a German shot putter.

I had to get over myself and my anxiety. "This will happen," Rob gently reminded me, fairly often. So I told myself, somewhat facetiously, to man up and face the future.

TESTOSTERONE IS A MIGHTY THING. Very mighty. The emotional changes seemingly created by the hormone compel me in my observations. In the bad old days, when we had a conflict or faced a difficult situation, Frankie would sometimes collapse in a fit of sobbing — inconsolable, anguished. It could last a whole evening or through the night. It was painful for him and painful to witness.

Now, especially if I am challenging a certain behaviour or attitude on Frankie's part, I am often met with defiance and sometimes a quick anger. Not tears. Not melancholy. Anger. He is very quick to anger now. He hastens to defend his rights. Is he just being a defiant teenager? Is he being difficult? Is it the hormones? Is it all of the above, as Rob insists?

When I was upset in the past, Frankie would often commiserate and console me in my unhappiness. Now a teary argument might prompt a quizzical look and the query, "Why can't we talk about this without crying?" or "I don't understand why you are crying, Mom." *Like a man,* I think with astonishment, *like a man he talks to me!* This shocks and amazes me.

In a way, this is reassuring if maddening at times. I need Frankie to be tough, I need him combat-ready, even a little insensitive to other's feelings, if he is to survive in this world, if he is to flourish in a sometimes hostile environment. And today, as things stand, I will take tough over sensitive to my needs any day.

# There Will Be Ink

✦

FRANKIE HAD BEEN ADVOCATING FOR a tattoo for several years and I thought this was in some way related to his transition. Being the horrid parents we were, we vetoed the idea. We told him he could not get one until he turned eighteen — in Ontario, those under that age are considered minors and are required to get parental permission before they can get a tattoo in a licensed parlour. With hindsight, I can issue this caution with certainty: Beware the parental veto, good people, beware.

Months before the time of Frankie's request, I noticed a very tiny, delicate image on the side of his palm. It was an equal sign. Blue ink. Somewhat innocuous. Less than a centimetre long. I thought nothing of it, but then I noticed that this image, one I had assumed was drawn in pen ink, was still there on his palm, weeks later. Frankie was always drawing on his arms and his legs, but a tiny light bulb went off in my head when I saw this image again weeks after the first time I had noticed it.

"That's not in blue pen ink is it?" I asked somewhat anxiously.

"Um … no," Frankie smiled sheepishly.

"What? Where did you get that??"

"My friend gave me a tattoo."

"*Your friend?* Does *your friend* run a *licensed* tattoo parlour?" I demanded.

"No … She did it at home. She does tattoos for her friends. It's the equal sign for equality. I thought you would like it."

"What the hell, Frankie! What did we say about tattoos until you are eighteen?!? Any other surprises for me?"

"Uhhh … just one more."

"Are you kidding me?"

He timidly pulled down his shirt collar and showed me a small blue tattoo on his collarbone. He is usually very covered up, many trans men are for obvious reasons. It was a delicate image of a wishbone about two centimetres in length, one side of the bone a little longer than the other. It was very pretty.

"I *thought* you would like it … it's about you and me. It's because you and I always break the wishbone together when we find it. You're the long bone, I'm the short bone."

He had an ingratiating shy smile on his face.

It was true. The breaking of the wishbone was our tradition. "Don't butter me up!" I fumed. "We told you Frankie, we told you the rule."

"But it's my life," he said sulkily.

*Not yet, it's not*, I thought.

"And I want a tattoo."

"At eighteen you can do whatever you want. But right now, not so much," I said.

ABOUT TWO MONTHS BEFORE HIS eighteenth birthday, Frankie boldly announced one night before he went to sleep that he still was going to get a tattoo. He had a very smug look on his face, which should have been the tip off for me.

*I know, I know!* I thought, inwardly sighing, *When you're eighteen.* I made nothing of his pronouncement as we had made Frankie promise not to do any more tattoos until he turned eighteen.

A scant week later, I was driving him to the subway. He was on his way to meet friends, he said. I asked him where he'd be. I wanted to have a sense of where he would be when out with his friends.

"Oh, yeah," he said casually before he got out of the car. "I'm probably getting a tattoo today."

"Wait. I thought we talked about this," I said, starting to feel the steam come out of my ears.

"But I told you last week I was going to." Indeed, he had.

"Yes, *and I told you*, you could get one in November, two months from now. Who's doing this tattoo? You can't get it done without my permission. You know that!"

"It's a friend of a friend."

"Oh no, you're not. Does this person run a licensed tattoo parlour?"

"No, he does it at home."

"What kind of tattoo?"

"A bee. You *love* bees," he said hopefully.

I did indeed love images of bees, just not on my kid. "A bee? Nope. No. No. You ... are ... not ..."

"But this guy is trans and it's important to me that he's the one who does it. I want it to be him."

"No … no …" I reiterated firmly.

There were tears and not a bit of yelling. A familiar face passed our car. I grimaced at the woman, but kept up my harangue that must have looked comical from her point of view.

In the midst of this, while we were still in the car, I called Frankie's dad and explained the situation. He immediately went on the offensive and got irate with Frankie. The thing that really incensed Rob, more than getting the tattoo, was that Frankie had promised not to get any more until he turned eighteen — it was the deceitfulness that bothered him and he said so in forceful terms. Thankfully, I could take the back seat on this one, as I was exhausted with this argument. I made Frankie promise me if I gave him any money that day he would not pay for a tattoo and he would wait until we researched a licensed parlour for him to go to. I promised I would do that for him. I have never broken my promises to him. He got out of the car and onto the subway, distressed and angry with us.

NO DOUBT THE QUESTION IS: What's the big deal here? Why not let him get another tattoo? All the cool kids were doing it. The real question, however, was why was it so important for him to get these tattoos when we, as his parents, were so vehemently opposed to them?

For me, it was the ongoing struggle of permitting Frankie to develop a separate, strong identity and controlling it somewhat so that it didn't spin into something where he could not assimilate into society. On a personal level, I kept futilely wondering why this child wanted to look so vastly different from me. From us. Even setting aside the obvious — he is trans and identifies as a boy, he wants to look like a boy — and we are cis (a gender identity that agrees with our societally recognized sex). But the piercings, the tattoos, they were alienating to me and to my generation, generally. They signified things that we're uneasy with. My younger and hipper friends were mystified by my conservative response. We, parents my age, will likely be the last untattooed generation once we are gone. Some might say good riddance with this narrow-minded attitude! But the tattoos, the piercings, made me feel more separated from Frankie. I was afraid they gave an impression of Frankie that was false — that he was tougher and seedier than he really was.

Frankie — and I think I understand the thought process a bit — felt different and he wanted that inner difference manifested in his outward appearance. *I am not like you. I need you to know that.* It was not unlike a certain period in my life when my hair was weird and my makeup was weird and my clothes were a bit weird. If you had asked me I would have said, "I dress this way because I like it." But it was more than that. I did not feel as one with my community — whether at school, or in my family, or in the working world. I felt distinct and I felt the need to set myself apart. As did Frankie.

We had these arguments all the time — why did he have to make himself so distinctly different? Didn't he have enough to contend with while transitioning? Why did he have to make it harder?

The real question was for me: How much change is too much?

# Oh Sonny Boy

❖

IMAGINE A BOXING RING. IN one corner is a battle-scarred and weary me — bruised, beaten up, definitely punching above her weight class. In the other corner is the larger, heavier, and younger opponent, the male pronouns — his and him. I battled this double-headed behemoth for months and the male pronouns pounded me mercilessly, relentlessly. In male pronouns' corner were Frankie and his coach, Rob. Both had a steely and determined look in their eyes. Male pronouns were out to kick my butt. Indisputably.

If only I would get on board, they thought. Rob was magnificent in this regard. Me, not so much. In fact, imprecations for me to *please use male pronouns and the noun son rather than daughter* often brought me to tears.

Rob had a lovely idea that he would take us to brunch in the Distillery District, where we would choose a new restaurant we had not been to before for Summerlicious, an annual festival in which participating Toronto restaurants offer reduced-price menu items. The Distillery district — a favourite haunt of ours — encompasses the beautifully restored red-brick, Victorian-era buildings of the Gooderham & Worts whiskey distillery in the downtown core of Toronto. The restaurant was beautiful, the staff pleasant, the buffet inviting. All was well until I took a photo of Frankie and Rob and asked if I could post it on Facebook. This caused a murmur of dissent and displeasure. Frankie didn't like the photo and exercised his veto, requesting it be excised. He was trying to control the presentation of his image, but I was not getting that yet. I misunderstood how important it was to him. It was irritating that I couldn't even get this right.

Earlier that day, Frankie had objected to the phrase "transgender daughter" on the blog I was writing. He said it should be "transgender son." He was correct, of course. That, coupled with earlier reprimands that I was repeatedly using "her" and "she" rather than "him" and "he" caused me to have a meltdown in the restaurant.

Female hormones might have had something to do with it. Somewhere between the first course of scrambled eggs and the dessert table, I burst into tears and asked Frankie to stop pecking away at me. "I know you are in transition," I said, almost shouting. "I'm in transition, too. Leave me alone, I'm trying! I'm trying! You are trying to get me to use the word son and I'm not ready, okay? I'm not ready!"

One thing I will say for Frankie, as soon as he saw I was in genuine distress, he dropped the pissy teenager routine and started acting like a reasonable adult human being toward me. I saw him melt before my eyes, dropping the attitude and expressing real concern. Poor Rob looked bereft and deflated.

"Well," he said in a forlorn tone. "This is really not how I expected lunch to go."

By this time, after my episode, we had all calmed down and I was feeling more reasonable. I understood Frankie's frustration. But I was honestly trying. My mistakes were honest ones and not an attempt to provoke or upset Frankie. But it was hard. For everyone.

Looking back, I realize how obtuse I was being. What Frankie was saying, without saying it exactly, was *You are not getting it — I'm your son now, not your daughter. I need you to refer to me as your son.*

It's like when I was explaining to a work colleague what was happening with the transition. Honestly trying to grapple with the information, she kept saying to me kindly, "So she wants you to call her *him?*" Even though I kept saying "he" and "him" in my explanation, it wasn't quite sinking in. Another casual friend said, "So, what am I supposed to call her again?" I wanted to shake him. Frankie previously *presented as female* and was *transitioning*, so the obvious choice is to refer to him as male and the usual he/his/him pronouns. I knew it was hard to wrap his head around this, but I wanted him to try.

But even I was messing up — especially with Frankie's friends, some of whom prefer neither male- or female-specific pronouns, but what they consider to be neutral pronouns, such as "they" and "them." The writer in me rebels against the use of the plural. Frankie resorted to writing out his friends' names and pronouns on a cheat sheet for me. In the middle of a particularly heated argument, he shouted angrily, "I am just trying *to educate you!*"

I stood my ground and pointed out a few things to him. I had not opposed the transition, although, yes, I had asked him to go slowly — which to some might seem like an abrogation of his rights, but it had seemed the right thing for us and him. I had not opposed the way he dressed or whom he slept with or his name change. I had supported him at school and with the family. I had shared the news of the transition with family, friends, neighbours, and colleagues, no matter how uncomfortable those conversations may have been for all involved. I had agreed to bear the cost of possible top surgery. I thought I had done everything I could possibly do as a supportive parent.

I felt like saying *Cut this old lady some slack. Your mother is old, she is tired, and very nearly beaten down by the inevitability of destiny.*

IN CASE THE READER HAS come to the conclusion that I've been earning my angel's wings and have been wearing a halo, let me take it off for a bit. It's heavy and perhaps a little tarnished. Maybe I'll shine it up and try it on again later. But now I have to tell you how unreasonable straight people can be with LGBTQ kids, even when they are the mothers of said LGBTQ kids.

Not long ago, I came home from a not-particularly-great day at work and then a not-particularly-great meeting with an organization I volunteer with. I was decidedly not in a good mood. I felt overtaxed, physically and emotionally drained, and I just wanted to crawl into bed without any drama or human interaction whatsoever. When I am excessively tired, I get a tad mean. I was getting ready for bed — I took my make up off, caught a bit of the news, read for a bit, then to sleep. Sugar, our half-Siamese, half tabby, crawled onto the headboard of the bed to watch me prepare for bed, his nightly ritual, my nightly companion.

Frankie came up to our third floor bedroom to say good-night, which is *his* nightly ritual, and mentioned that two friends were coming over the next evening. "And, by the way," he said lightly, "they don't identify as male or female, so please don't refer to them as girls. Use the words *they* or *them*. Please."

"What?" I snapped. "They can't pick one — male *or* female?"

"That's *rude*." Frankie responded stiffly, taken aback.

"Christ," I shot back. "I have enough trouble remembering to use male pronouns with *you*." I turned my back on him roughly.

Frankie left the room in a huff, presumably to gripe to his dad about what a jerk I was being. He was not incorrect. I went to bed crossly — no apologies, no regrets. When Rob came up later to go to bed, I could sense that he knew what I had said to Frankie. Wisely, he chose not to bring it up.

At two forty-five a.m. I woke up — full of anxiety, hyper alert, physically uncomfortable. This is not uncommon for me. I know how nights like this generally evolved — tossing, turning, sighing, disturbing Rob — so I snuck into the middle bedroom on the second floor to try and settle down. The extra bedroom, the room that was meant to be the baby's room, is next to Frankie's room. The floors creaked as I entered the room. To my surprise, Frankie was up. He quietly crawled into bed with me. He couldn't sleep either. Unfortunately, my child has inherited my sleep problems. Then the kitten Louie crawled in beside Frankie. Louie was happily purring, nestled against Frankie's tummy, paws stretched out, entirely buried under the duvet. We were like three spoons in the bed, with Louie as the smallest spoon.

"I'm sorry," I said with real regret. "That was really rude."

"It's okay," Frankie said gently. I wrapped my arm around his torso and hugged him.

"You know that your friends are welcome here any time, right?"

"Yes, I know," he replied.

I felt there was still a deep chasm between us. I don't know if we can ever bridge it. I'm not sure that Frankie will ever understand how upset and confused I am by the transition and I am worried I will never understand the pressure he is under to find a way of being that others will accept and respect. But he is trying and I am trying.

We lay together for a while. Louie started purring. Very loudly. *At least one living creature in this house is happy*, I thought. But at this close range Louie's purring sounded like a car motor running on the right side of the bed. I loved the little guy, but jeez …

"I can't sleep, Frankie. Louie's too loud."

"I'll take him into my bedroom, Mom. It's okay. Good-night." He gave me a loving hug and left, kitten perched in his arms.

It took a while, but eventually I fell fitfully asleep. Rob came and woke me for work the next morning.

"I was mean to Frankie last night," I said, regretfully, over our usual breakfast of tea with milk and toast.

"I know," Rob said. "I spoke to him last night."

"What did you say to him?" I asked shamefacedly.

"'Mom's having a bad time right now and said the wrong thing. You know how sometimes you just say the wrong thing and then you regret it?'"

"What did Frankie say?"

"'Yeah,'" Frankie had conceded. He knew.

"That was it?" I asked.

"Yup." End of discussion. Mercifully.

Rob asked me if I had seen the link that Frankie had sent us by email the night before, presumably after my snippy remarks to him. I said no. He started to describe the video but was getting choked up as he spoke of it. The way he was describing it was affecting me, too, but I said nothing. I was tired and couldn't afford any more drama that morning. Frankie was sleeping in because he had a late class, so I didn't disturb him as I left for work.

When I got to work I saw that Frankie had sent us both a link to a video of a poetry reading. The poem, "A Letter to the Girl I Used to Be," was read by a young poet named Ethan Smith. I clicked on the link. Ethan was a trans man — he used to be Emily and now he is Ethan.

Dear Emily,

Every time I watch baseball
a voice I no longer recognize whispers:

*Ethan, do you remember?*
*When you were gonna be the first girl to play in the major leagues?*
*Seattle Mariners. Rally cap.*

But to be honest, Emily, I don't.
Dad told me that like it was someone else's bedtime story.

But I do know you had that drive,
didn't let anyone tell you to wear shorts above your knees,
didn't care if boys thought your hair fell on your shoulders
      just right.
But with girls, sleepovers meant the space
between your shoulder and hers was a 6-inch fatal territory.

The year you turned eleven was the first time you said
      out loud
that you didn't want to live anymore.
In therapy, you said you wouldn't make it to 21.
On my 21st birthday, I thought about you,
you were right.

At nineteen, you started to fade.
I tried to cross you out, like a line in my memoir
I wished I could erase completely.
And maybe I'm misunderstanding the definition of death,
but even though parts of you still exist, you are not here,
most of my friends have never heard your name until now.

I've been trying to write this letter for six months,
I still can't decide if it should be an apology or not.


But now you will never hear 'Emily Smith' announced at
a college graduation, get married, give birth.
When the prescribed testosterone started taking effect
my body stopped producing the potential for new life
    every month.
I thought about your children, how I wanted them too.


I let a doctor remove your breasts so that I could stand
    up straighter.
Now even if I somehow had those children,
I wouldn't be able to nourish them.
My body is obsolete,
scarred cosmetic, but never C-section.


I was four days late,
they will never be grandparents.
I was one week late,
they will never hold their lover's sleeping figure.
I was eleven days late,
they will never breathe in a sunset and sunrise in the
    same night.
I was two weeks late,
they will never learn to jump rope.
I was three weeks late,
they will never shout *Watch Mommy! Watch me on the slide!*

I was two months late,
a piece of us will never wrap their arms around our leg
    for comfort,
or just to keep them from falling down.

And I am sorry, that this process is so slow,
and all you can do is wonder if you ever had a place.
You did. You still do. Don't forget that.

Yours,
Ethan

p.s.
I never hated you.

At my desk, with my child's message staring me in the face in the form of this poem and with my colleagues quietly working around me, the tears slowly slid down my face and I thought, *there's nothing worse than weeping at work.*

# A Girl Like Me

✦

FRANKIE OFTEN PICKED THROUGH ROB'S clothes from the 1970s and '80s that are kept in the old walnut armoire in our bedroom. They're too vintage for someone Rob's age to wear, but too cool to throw out, so we have squirreled them away. Frankie favours Rob's ripped punk T-shirts with political or nonsensical slogans and band names, Rob's safety-pin-encrusted jean jacket, which is slowly disintegrating from its use and love and age, and some bits from the costume jewellery we both possess. This sometimes filled me with dismay, although it makes perfect sense. Frankie loves his father and his father's style and wanted to emulate him in every way. And Rob is a good role model — handsome, cool, and stylish.

This sent a wave of melancholy through me. What did I want Frankie to look like? What did I want Frankie to be? Clearly, I wanted *someone* to be a girl like me. Although Frankie shares many of my emotional characteristics — he's passionate, loyal, anti-authority, needy, quick-tempered — I wanted, of course, that he would look like me and want to share my tastes in clothing, appearance, hairstyle, grooming. A smaller, prettier version of me. This was what I knew I wanted before his transition.

My reading in this area suggested that the parent who feels that his, or her, gender is being rejected by the trans child is the parent most conflicted about the transition. In Frankie's pre-transition days, it gave me a small soupcon of satisfaction when Frankie picked through my jewellery box with curiosity looking for a silver ring or bracelet to wear. As laborious as the process was, I liked helping her dry and straighten her then long, thick, dark hair that resembled mine. I enjoyed the pretty bangles, short neat sweaters, and wands of black mascara that we shared. Those days were long gone. The last thing Frankie wanted was to resemble his mother. It is silly to assume that because your child does not want to physically resemble you, they are rejecting you. But I couldn't help feeling that way at times.

You may have lost a daughter but you have gained a son, I am told. I imagined that people thought these words were comforting. But what if I never imagined having a son? My relations with him were slowly shifting in subtle ways — as they must — and yet I felt resentment that I had to change my perspective with him. Now I had to stop and think, *If I had a nineteen-year-old son, a cis gender son, would I insist on picking him up from his girlfriend's home after midnight? Would I feel comfortable enough to crawl into bed with him for a cuddle? Would I condition myself to do the heavy lifting of day-to-day chores to spare my son the labour? Would I change in front of him?* Honestly, no.

With a cis gender son, I would find my overprotection emasculating. May I use the word *emasculating* still? I would consider my need for a cuddle a bit odd — moms shouldn't be lying in bed with teenage sons. I would feel uncomfortable if he saw me undressed or walked into the bathroom while I was in there. I would expect my son to carry the groceries, take out the garbage, walk his girlfriend home, be protective and chivalrous towards me and other women, open doors for his girlfriend, be vigilant and courteous towards his female cousins and female relations.

When Rob wondered aloud why Frankie did not extend the courtesy of walking a female friend to the streetcar stop or accompany his girlfriend all the way home on a late night date, I want to remind him that Frankie did not suddenly grow six inches in height or develop massive muscles. He is still the same shape, size, and weight — he would be no more prepared to defend an imperilled female than I was. Frankie was not a physical person, nor was he ever involved in a fist fight, nor had he been in a physical altercation. Rob was expecting Frankie to act like a courteous gentleman, to be able to protect his girlfriend. I was not.

I would expect a certain amount of boorish, immature behaviour, too, that I wouldn't have tolerated from a daughter because I have an image of what an ideal daughter should be that is distinctly different from what I imagine for an ideal son. Frankie's transition necessitated a revolution in my thinking: less stereotypic, less rigid regarding gender roles. I had to learn to be more genderfluid in my expectations of my son.

# Turning On and Tuning In to Trans TV

✧

In the summer of 2014, my offspring co-founded and co-created a collaborative YouTube video series about transmasculine people — people who were designated female at birth (a.k.a *dfab*) and have since transitioned socially and/or medically. The series was made up of approximately fourteen transmasculine people. The purpose of the video series was to help other transmasculine people through the process of transitioning. Frankie met another trans man on Tumblr and they thought this up together. The videos are archived on YouTube. This I did not learn right away, as Frankie was self-conscious about discussing it.

I asked Frankie about the origin of the videos. He told me that twice a day, one of the fourteen transmasculine people they had invited to participate would talk about their experiences. They varied in age from thirteen to twenty-seven years of age. They only went by their first names on the videos, including Frankie. They covered a wide range of topics — when they came out, how they came out, to whom they came out, their sexual orientation, the physical process of transitioning, how they felt about transitioning. They were branching out to discuss activities like sports — a special challenge if you are a trans boy or trans man who wishes to play on an all-male team comprised of cis men.

I made the mistake of texting Frankie one day to ask him about the series. He was out with friends celebrating a birthday. As a mother, I confess to having exquisite timing. I wanted to write about the series, but as I had not seen it — I was forbidden to do so — I didn't know how to write about it. Frankie called me immediately, very anxious, thinking that I had somehow glimpsed it or that someone I knew had seen him online and told me about it.

"Relax!" I said. "I just wanted to talk to you about it when you got home. What's the big deal? You're not doing anything that would freak me out, right? I mean ... *right?*" I was hoping there was no flesh involved.

"Of course not!" he said, miffed. "It's just that it's private." And private it was to remain.

Frankie also runs a blog where non-binary people — whose gender identities are not exclusively masculine or feminine — post their selfies. He describes it as a sort of support system.

I inadvertently saw a clip of a video that Frankie was recording one day, using my computer in the early days of this YouTube video series. He left the screen open in the living room. I clicked on video image. Simple as that. Frankie's beanie-clad head and hip-nerdy glasses popped up on the screen. The video was shot in his bedroom and he was addressing the camera very naturally, very confidently. I listened for a moment or two because I did not know what I was looking at. Frankie spoke. "You know my mom's all like upset that she is losing her little girl," he said in a droll voice. "The thing is ... there never was a little girl." I immediately clicked off, embarrassed that I had stumbled upon this. But what struck me was the lack of compassion in his voice. As if, *no big thing*, you thought you gave birth to a girl but, hey, it's a boy so *deal with it*. We had a little discussion afterwards about that video.

I REASONED AT FIRST THAT if Frankie truly wanted privacy, he should have refrained from using his parents' technology without permission and he should not have left it in full view of said parents. He is entitled to his private musings, even if I find them to be mildly alarming and insensitive. More importantly, the trans child presumably has had a much longer time to deal with this new information about being trans than the parent has. I would have appreciated a more sympathetic tone about how I felt and how I reacted to the news. However, I am the adult and it's my job to educate him.

I understand that for parents of trans children in comparable situations it is indeed a very big deal. A parent of a trans child has the right to be confused, hurt, upset, nervous, anxious, even angry, at how things have transpired. *That is our right*. However, it is not our right to thwart, undermine, shame, harm or belittle the trans child. It is not our right to actively work against our children's express wishes about the transition because we feel confusion, pain, nervousness, embarrassment, anger, shame. For those who feel that they can't proceed: it is your job to protect your child against all the elements in society that threaten them. This includes reactionary societal norms, religious persecution, bigotry, sexism, and homophobia. This is what the parent of the trans child has signed up for — the care and nurturing of a child under all circumstances, against all adversity.

Frankie and I talk about how often people congratulate the parent who provides a loving, accepting home for a trans child. "It's like they are congratulating you for acting like a decent human being," he said. He's exactly right. That's how the parents of trans kids should be behaving, as difficult as that may be at times.

Once I was berating Frankie for what I perceived as his lack of respect and appreciation for what his father and I had done for him regarding the transition. This pressed a hot button for him and he burst into tears, which is rare since he began HRT.

"I do appreciate what you've done. I do know I am lucky. I have thanked you, Mom. More than once. What do you want me to do, write a thank-you card?"

He was right. Again. What was I expecting from him? Demonstrate support, show your love for your child, but never forget that to respond humanely towards the trans child is the absolute minimum that you should do. It doesn't make you a hero.

When I hear some of the stories of the lives of Frankie's trans and queer friends, I am furious. There are stories of kids being forced by a parent to move out; sometimes being physically assaulted by their parents; facing restrictive and abusive rules for living in their parents' homes because they are out and the parent does not, cannot, accept this; absent fathers who have disappeared from the kids' lives. These actions have horrendous consequences for teenagers — sometimes leading to homelessness, substance abuse, alcoholism, poverty, inability or disinclination to continue school, engagement in abusive, manipulative relationships with others, alienation from the family structure, and worse.

Who are we to judge these parents? some ask. Let me take that on. I will judge them. Regardless of their religious faith, the "values" of their community, their personal feelings of disapproval or disgust, their fear of society's judgment, regardless of all these factors — they are terrible parents who are abdicating their most important obligation as human beings: to care for and nurture their child regardless of circumstances. I am uncomfortable, Rob is uncomfortable, *we* are uncomfortable, being congratulated for acting like human beings and doing the right thing. It's the absolute minimum that the parent of a trans child should and can do.

# We All Have Our Mice

✦

I HAVE BEEN ANGRY, EXHAUSTED, combative, harsh, unkind, argumentative. Sometimes I have not been respectful of Rob's feelings and needs. I felt at times that I have had nothing left to give to anyone but Frankie and to the preservation of his health and wellbeing. That is not how I wanted to live my life. Obviously when you meet the man you will marry and bear a child with, you cannot foresee what challenges your life will hold for you — a crisis that will test the bonds of your marriage and rock its foundation. Your life with your child — a wondrous, magical, joyous time — may turn frightening and unstable when you realize that your child is in jeopardy. I never wanted to be the wife, in this situation, who turns to her husband and says, or wearily implies, *You are my last priority — it's my child, my family, my work, then you. In that order.* I did not want to be that person, but, sometimes, regretfully, I feel that I have acted like that person.

Rob and I respond differently to the stresses that have come with Frankie's depression and then his transition. When

I am preoccupied with worry about Frankie, my laser focus is on his health and emotional wellbeing — sometimes to the detriment of the other things in my life and other people's feelings. My memory regarding day-to-day issues is affected too. I am usually highly organized, reaching an annoying OCD level of management of my personal affairs, family business, and work life. Like most women with partners and children, I work full time and manage the social schedule for the family. I manage all the birthdays and special events, buy most of the gifts, organize family events, send cards to friends and family members, remind my nearest and dearest to call other family members in times of need or trouble. I ensure people get to, or make, their medical and dental appointments, get their prescriptions filled, nag about daily exercises, ask people to periodically clean up, purge their items, donate things. I volunteer with various organizations. That's not extraordinary — that's just what we do as mothers, as wives. But when I am stressed, I double down on my responsibilities. I take on more assignments and extra duties at work, I find additional causes to volunteer for, I read more ambitiously. It's not because I'm virtuous or highly competent. It's because I'm terrified of what is going on in my life and I am afraid to face it. *Why am I doing this? Why all this extra work when my plate is so full?* I often think. *Because I'm trying not to remember what I am upset about.*

Rob has a different approach. When Rob is upset, he focuses on the small things that annoy him in the maintenance of the household. I surmise that this is because these things are easier to control, to manage, than the big issues. I go off like a firecracker, Rob simmers like a pot. The firecracker blows up. What does the pot do? The pot bubbles slowly and then fumes furiously.

Rob and I end up fighting about the bread crumbs I left on the kitchen table and the faucet that I did not securely tighten and the house keys I left in the door and the cap on the bottle I did not close tightly enough and the shoes I left in his path to the kitchen and the cat's litter box I forgot to clean. I lose my temper when he is impatient about these things because I am thinking, *Do you understand what is going on? Do you get what our child is experiencing? What we are* all *experiencing? Why are you harassing me about this?* Of course he understands the pressure we are under, but I think in order for him to continue on in a calm and rational manner in the face of the stress and anxiety, he has to keep the small things in order.

This pattern of behaviour reminds me of the year I miscarried our first child, eight weeks into the pregnancy. This was fourteen months before Frankie was born. We were trying to get pregnant again and it was a stressful, decidedly unromantic, and challenging time in our marriage — simulating sexual love on a schedule is, surprisingly, not an inspiring thing for men I am told. But what I most remember from that year about our relationship was Rob's obsession with catching the mice that had invaded the kitchen in our first home, a little row house with a shabby, unrenovated kitchen and an ever-damp basement. Rob talked incessantly about how to rid the house of the mice. He was making me anxious, talking about the number of mice we had, how they should be caught, what was the most humane way, where they had come from, how awful it was to kill them, and if they returned, what methods he would use the second time around. I listened to him, growing impatient and then increasingly furious. Could he not see my disinterest? My growing boredom? I felt like yelling, "We just lost a child, we are trying to get pregnant again and you are talking about mice. *Mice!*" But that's how he coped, that's how *we* coped. We all have our mice. And we deal with them in various ways.

I FIND IT CURIOUS THAT Rob and I have reversed our parental roles somewhat now. When Frankie was struggling to come out and was not able to function in a healthy fashion, when he was depressed and unhappy, I was the more sensitive one; I was more forbearing, the one who strove to understand what was happening. Now it is Rob who is accommodating and sensitive to his needs. It is Rob who accompanied Frankie to the doctor to learn how to do the testosterone injections. It is Rob who taught Frankie how to shave. It is Rob who expressed sympathy and sensitivity when Frankie bemoaned his height or wanted to change his physical look.

Now it is me who is obstinate, a bit insensitive, prone to outbursts of incomprehension and bewilderment, as Rob once was when Frankie could not rise from his bed, could not attend school or function normally. I am the one who is mystified, belligerent at times, withdrawn, resentful.

Once, Rob confronted me directly about our difficulties after a particularly challenging week of emotional outbursts and petty fights. I was unhappy and teary, fearful of the next stage. Frankie urged me to be honest with Rob about what was troubling me.

"I think you are angry with me and I think I know why," he said. "You are angry because we are not on the same page about the transition." The look on his face said I don't think you will admit to this.

"Exactly," I said acidly, and without an ounce of remorse.

How could I tell him — when he said "son," when he said "he" and "him" in accordance with Frankie's express wishes, I thought "Traitor." Almost every time. I felt like he had betrayed me. Betrayed us. Betrayed what we had. But I knew this was wrong. Rob was doing exactly the right thing.

Now I wear the hat of the bad guy — the one who does not want Frankie to change, who is secretly, or openly, resentful of the smallest deviation in him and his physical appearance. And it feels good in a way. I don't have to be vigilant each and every moment. I don't have to be patient, forbearing, kind at all times. I know Rob is there to protect Frankie, encourage him, advise him. I know Frankie will make it through even if I grumble a bit or if I am weepy at the thought of what is ahead. Rob will be there as will I. I am not alone and, more importantly, Frankie is not alone.

In times of high anxiety I have to remind myself that I have indeed won the husband lottery, as one friend gleefully put it. He is a warm, loving, intelligent being full of patience. And he is a bottomless well of love for both Frankie and me.

# A Tale of Two Families

❖

PART ONE

Our families have been mostly supportive, if quietly so, aside from a resounding silence from some portions of the extended family. Then again, I wasn't expecting a parade to celebrate the transition. You have to admit, it's a lot to take in, especially for older members of the family who are puzzled, upset, or confused by the whole concept of gender dysphoria. Frankie has set the agenda from day one in discussing the transition openly. He decided when we should tell our immediate families and then requested that we tell our extended families and neighbours.

I wanted to visit an elderly relative I knew was uneasy with the transition. She lived in a small town that I would not consider a bastion of liberal values. I think I can safely say that she knows no one who is openly gay, much less openly trans. When I called to confirm the dinner we were to have together that night, I asked if Frankie could bring his new girlfriend and she immediately said yes. I asked her gently, "You know what I mean when I say girlfriend, right?" "Yesssss," she said in a somewhat impatient tone. *She knew.*

I was aware that Danny, her son, would be there with his two teenage children so I wanted to check to see how he felt about it. I called him and sensed that he was upset. He sounded edgy and preoccupied. I asked him if he was okay with the visit. He shot back, "Why are you asking me? You should be checking with my mother." "I did," I said, a little shocked by the vehemence of his remark. I told him that she said it was okay. "Oh, what did you expect her to say?" he asked me sarcastically.

He said that his family was not entirely comfortable with meeting this new girlfriend. They supported Frankie, they loved Frankie, but ...

Taken aback, I said somewhat angrily, "So, what are you telling me? You accept Frankie, you will respect his choices, but he can't live as a human being, can't bring a girlfriend for dinner, can't live a normal life because it's too upsetting for you to acknowledge?"

Was he really so naive as to believe that he and his family never cross paths with a gay or trans person in their workplace, school, neighbourhood? If so, how had that impacted his life negatively? Let me tell you ... not at all.

As calmly as I could, I told him if he couldn't accept this part of Frankie's life then he was forcing me to say that we couldn't be part of his. I love this relation, but just then I wanted to reach through the phone and throttle him.

He said heatedly, "Oh, is that an ultimatum?"

"Take it any way you like," I replied coldly.

It went back and forth and back and forth testily — his

defence was something along the lines of *You may think we're bigots but we're not. I know you think because we don't live in Toronto we're not as sophisticated as you guys. I can't force my family to accept things they aren't comfortable with.* Before I knew it the conversation was over and we hung up, both very unhappy with the outcome.

I was unsure what to do. To this family member, the news about the transition seemed less disturbing than the idea that Frankie had a girlfriend and that they were about to meet her. Perhaps this was physical proof that Frankie was not what they thought he once was? I was utterly confused by the upset. This attitude was the very reason I left my own hometown, I thought bitterly.

Rob had been listening the whole time and said, "Maybe we shouldn't go."

"You're right," I said. "I really don't feel good about it now." But I was very disappointed by the response. More like furious.

"Well, let's not overreact. Let me speak to Danny again," Rob said. Rob called him back and left a message and then Danny called back and left a message. They were unable to connect directly and, frustratingly, they went back and forth all afternoon on their cells.

Eventually, Danny texted me. *It's fine, everything's okay, come!* But I was still fuming and confused as to how to proceed. Hours passed. I did not respond to Danny's text as I mulled over what to do.

Then Danny texted me. *You know, I have an iPhone and I can see that you read my text, but you're not getting back to me.* That made me laugh — although I don't think he was being funny, I think he was angry. But I was still undecided.

Finally, Rob and Danny connected on the phone. Danny commented to my husband, "I was trying to explain my position to her and she *went all mama bear on me*." Rob communicated this to me later laughingly. *Damn right*, I thought. *Don't mess with Frankie. Don't mess with my kid.*

In the end Danny said, "Come. Everything is okay. Come." I felt badly that I was putting this strain on the family. But I only felt badly a little; it was more like I was vastly disappointed in him. We did go that night for dinner. I'm not going to say that the vibe wasn't weird — it was. There were a lot of strained smiles and some semi-cold responses to our presence. But they were trying and we were trying and the night passed without incident. No further drama ensued. And that's pretty much the best I could ask for.

PART TWO

Frankie asked that his dad tell his side of the family about the transition and about his desire to be addressed with male pronouns. Rob's side of the family has had more contact with Frankie than my side of the family — we all live in Toronto — and were more likely to see him and notice the changes. It was a judicious move on his part. Frankie was a darling in my husband's family: first grandchild, first granddaughter. Rob's family would fight and argue amongst themselves to hold her, to change her, to care for her. They followed me into the bedroom when I changed her. They grabbed her from my arms the moment I entered the house we were visiting just after she was born.

Rob was right on it. For him, it was an enormous relief

to be open about what was happening. These are not family members we see frequently, but we see them more often than my side of the family. Rob wrote a detailed email to the family — aunts and uncles and first cousins. He explained that Frankie had been quite ill, had gone through ongoing physical changes, and there was a specific reason for that. He asked that they respect Frankie's decision to be referred to with male pronouns and by a male identity.

Those several people who responded — all of them first cousins and their partners, and only one elderly aunt from the older generation of aunts and uncles — responded promptly and supportively. They expressed great kindness and respect in their emails. I was very touched. From the rest, there was a vast, empty silence — one that has still not been bridged.

PART THREE

This next part of coming out to all was very hard for me, although it remained a mystery as to why this would be so for Frankie. Frankie was adamant that I contact my extended family on my mother's side to tell them what was happening. In December of each year we always have a huge Christmas celebration in my hometown. My cousins rent a hall and all of the relations — grandparents, children and partners, grand-children and their partners — gather for a multi-course dinner in a decorated hall, awaiting a special visit from Santa Claus (courtesy of one of my male cousins in a rented suit). The generation of first cousins, my generation, range in age from their early thirties to late fifties. The grandchildren range from toddlers to young adults in their first jobs and relationships. This is a gathering of approximately one hundred or so people.

The idea of speaking to my first cousins about the transition filled me with an unnamed dread. I feared their judgment and scorn. It's not that they were harsh, mean, or unforgiving people, but this was so far beyond most people's daily experiences that I feared they would be alarmed and disturbed by my news. Most of my cousins had remained in my hometown or moved into the suburbs of Toronto — Oakville, Burlington, Mississauga. We are friendly and warm with each other, but we are not close.

But another thing — and I admit my fear was entirely selfish — I had been a troubled and unhappy teenager who made many mistakes, many of which were witnessed by my cousins. Would they, mistakenly of course, attribute Frankie's journey to some weird, unorthodox element of my parenting? Would they hold me responsible for something I could not control, nor wished to have control over? When Frankie bravely pushed me to contact them, these are the thoughts that plagued me. But I gave myself a deadline. I would contact my cousins in November of 2014, one month before the Christmas party. Let the chips fall where they may.

I contacted my cousins on Facebook asking for their personal emails and telling them that I had some news to share. Some quickly sent me their emails as well as concerned replies asking if everything was okay. I sent a detailed email about Frankie from work at noon. It spoke of Frankie's struggles, his emotional history, his progress since he came out, his improving health status.

And then I waited — sweating, vaguely nauseous and anxious. A few quiet hours passed. I could imagine all five sets of siblings — the offspring of my mother's four sisters and lone brother — texting and sending emails to each other in absolute wonderment and curiosity. Then the emails started to trickle in. They were loving, supportive, some explicitly declared their love and support for Frankie. Some offered to assist us in any way. Some praised Frankie, others praised us for our support. Almost all responded. My anxiety, which had built and built for months, blessedly dissipated. How they would attempt to explain this momentous change to their parents or children, I couldn't begin to think about.

My heart was filled with enormous love for them in directly facing this change with kindness and understanding.

# Just a Brilliant Disguise

❖

AS THE TIME APPROACHED FOR Frankie to plan and commit to the top surgery, I found myself increasingly fragile. I, a mother who cannot look at a cut on Frankie's body without feeling queasy, now had to contemplate what my child's body would be like after a double mastectomy. That's the truth of it — that's what would be a consequence of the surgery. Sometimes, I would think it was too much to bear.

There are certain songs that seem to capture what you are going through at a particular time in your life. Rob introduced me to a song called "Hero" by the American band Family of the Year. The song was featured in the film *Boyhood*. I didn't think much of it initially. The words just glided by me until I listened to it more carefully after Rob played it repeatedly. Now I played it incessantly, too. And in no way do I believe the song was written to reflect the feelings of a trans kid, but it caught me at a time when I was struggling with Frankie's plans to hasten his transition. I kept imagining this kid beseeching me to let him be himself:

Does my discomfort and fear trump Frankie's anxiety about his body? What do I want to condemn him to? A life of self-hate and loathing because I am afraid, anxious, angry? Do I want him to continue with this charade that society, and I, have imposed on him — that he be what he appears to be externally and not what he is inside?

We had ferocious fights. I was accused of misgendering Frankie, of not trying hard enough, of refusing to see him as a boy. He asked me at one point if I saw him as a boy. I said, "Do you want me to be honest?"

"I already know," he said bitterly and turned away. He said that I hated the word boy and son when applied to him. I rarely used those words with him then, words that he longed to hear: my son, my boy, man. He was not entirely incorrect.

When I discussed my ambivalence with Rob, he too grew irritated with me. I wasn't coming around, I was hurting Frankie. I was putting my feelings first but Frankie's had to be paramount. This all may have been true but I could not be accused of not trying to be sympathetic or open. The song "Hero" made me feel like the true phony I was when we, as parents, were lauded for our understanding, our courage — so inclusive and so respectful when I know what it has cost me, what it has cost us.

After a stormy weekend of fighting and emotional out bursts on all sides, I finally came to the realization that my resistance was causing Frankie much unwarranted pain. I had to stop dragging my feet on the issue of top surgery. When I returned to work, I did my due diligence. I investigated the clinic that Frankie wanted to go to, even though I was uneasy going to the clinic myself for a formal appointment. I left that to Rob and Frankie. I searched for legal cases or suits against the clinic and the head surgeon. We discussed the merits of going through CAMH versus this clinic. CAMH's position on this issue mystified me: if a patient was approved through their assessment process, the patient had to go to a clinic in Quebec for the surgery. There was only one approved option for surgery. The advantage was that OHIP would pay for it. There were disadvantages. Frankie would have to go out of province and he was unimpressed with the work they had done on FTM patients — the evidence of which were in scarce supply on the Internet. Not so with the Ontario clinic: ringing endorsements from patients, examples of their surgical work, an overall positive rating from trans patients.

While contemplating whether to proceed, I thought about how powerless trans teenagers are. They require their parents' signature and approximately one hundred and eighty dollars to change their names legally in Ontario. They require their parents' permission in high school to have the manner in which they are addressed changed on their documentation or to use the washroom they feel most comfortable in. A teenager needs money to buy the clothes and accessories that will alter his/her appearance. A teenager requires parental drug benefits programs to cover the expenses of hormone treatment that can be onerous financially — the cost of Lupron, to suppress menstruation, runs into the many thousands of dollars over a number of months, the cost of testosterone to enhance masculine characteristics for FTM. A teenager needs his parents' permission to have surgery, if underage, and most decidedly his or her parents' money to go to a clinic not sanctioned by OHIP for surgery.

How frustrated would that make you? How deep a sense of powerlessness? How angry? I could not keep prevaricating. I had to commit to the surgery. I knew I was the one slowing down the process. It had to be done in the summer so that it would not interfere with Frankie's school year. I asked Frankie to come downstairs to talk to us so that I could tell him. I said it was about the surgery. He scooted down quickly and plopped on the couch. I said that he should book the surgery with the clinic. I said we shouldn't waste any more time. After all, I said, he had been asking for the surgery for the last two-and-a-half years, since he had come out at sixteen. He was not legally an adult then. He was now. We knew how important it was to him. He looked at me in wonder and said with a dazed look, "Is this real?"

Yes son, it's real.

ONCE I BLURTED OUT TO Frankie, "Please don't change ..." as we cuddled together after a long day. In my mind I was thinking, *Always stay this sweet*. But obviously there was also a subtext — the desire that Frankie not physically change. He knew immediately what I meant. He put an arm around me and tried to reassure me, "I won't be a different person after I start testosterone, Mom, I promise." But how could he not?

I admit I was frightened of what was to come — HRT and top surgery. Frankie was adamant. The name change was hard, but not insurmountable. The switch to male pronouns was very difficult to navigate but, again, not insurmountable. But the next phase — the physical changes to come — rattled me. To contemplate that soft, beautiful face covered with stubble or to hear that lovely voice deepen was challenging.

And then there was the top surgery. I don't think I ever had a moment — aside from the first uncomfortable year of development when I was attracting unwanted attention from boys and men — where I regretted my breast size. Let the sporty girls moan that it interfered with soccer or jogging. I never faced these anxieties or self-hate. I remembered Frankie's queries and anticipation about her own physical development when Frankie identified as a girl, and it was not with horror. There was expectancy and wonder. Was his feeling false then and genuine now? Or vice versa? Or might both be true?

If we proceeded — and it seemed based on Frankie's intense feelings that we must — were we pursuing the right course? The idea of changing any part of him physically was painful and upsetting to me for, as every mother feels, my child was perfect in my eyes. Wondrous, beautiful, flawless, without parallel. This made standing on the sidelines especially difficult.

I COULD NOT BEAR TO attend the preliminary appointment with the plastic surgeon to discuss Frankie's double mastectomy. Images of it kept me up at night and would suddenly reduce me to tears in solitary moments. The surgeon Frankie had requested was well-respected and had numerous testimonials from trans boys and trans men who were satisfied with the results of the surgery, according to the surgeon's website and the trans kids to whom Frankie had reached out online. He had patients from around the country and the world. This was the surgeon Frankie had contacted when he first came out to us at sixteen in the fall of 2012. Back then, I was so distraught that I just shut down the conversation immediately and refused to discuss having a surgical consultation.

Rob went to the preliminary meeting with the surgeon to discuss the procedure, the process of recovery, and the cost. Because we had not gone through the lengthy assessment at the Gender Identity Clinic at the Centre for Addiction and Mental Health (we'd done the assessment for mental health, but not surgery) we had to pay for the surgery ourselves rather than have it paid for by OHIP.

THE EVALUATION PROCESS FOR GENDER reassignment surgery at CAMH, as it was described then, was quite extensive and there was a long waiting list. CAMH is affiliated with one institution, and only one, that performs mastectomies for trans boys and men; that clinic is located, inexplicably, in Quebec. This is problematic, on so many levels, for trans patients in Ontario, especially those who do not have substantial financial means. Families accompanying a young trans patient must travel out of province and find accommodations while the surgery is conducted. Frankie was adamant he did not want to do that. And the CAMH process was slow; some might say that CAMH was being careful and judicious in the processing of potential surgical patients, but for those who were adamant that they wanted the surgery the pace of the process was perceived as tortuous and cruel.

I kept thinking about those kids who couldn't afford the surgery, who didn't have the emotional or financial support of their parents. How dispiriting this would be for them. But, in a manner, I was glad we had to pay for it ourselves, because I didn't want anyone attacking Frankie with the argument that "as a taxpayer" they didn't want to pay for his surgery. My not-so-secret desire was that such people would just leave everyone who has to endure this alone. It is a difficult, emotionally challenging process as it is.

For weeks after Frankie knew we had agreed to let him proceed with the surgery, he had been advocating to start a crowdfunding venture on social media to help him raise the funds from friends and allies in the trans community. Rob said no immediately. He was opposed to the idea. It's not that we had the cash on hand, but we have enough financial resources that we could borrow that amount. But Frankie felt very guilty about the amount required and wanted to help out in some way. I convinced Rob to let Frankie do it. I was sure that Frankie would only raise a few hundred dollars and that would be the end of it. He would feel better and then we could proceed. I asked Frankie to block all family members and adults close to us on social media so they wouldn't feel obliged to contribute. What happened was quite unexpected.

Frankie's friends told, or showed, their parents the site and the parents started contributing to the fund. These were our friends and neighbours and in one instance an extended family member Frankie had forgot to block. In the end, Frankie raised three thousand dollars — a third of the amount required — and we had to cap the fund. And when one acquaintance, a friend of Frankie's friend, left a sarcastic comment on his Facebook page about how she had worthier things to do with her money, Frankie shot right back and put her in her place about how expensive and difficult it was for trans kids to afford the surgery they so desperately wanted.

A FEW DAYS BEFORE THE procedure there was a pre-surgery appointment. Rob had agreed to attend with Frankie, but had a last minute rush assignment for work and could not make it, so I went instead. The plastic surgeon was located in Mississauga, a suburb about thirty miles west of Toronto. I could see Rob vacillating. *Can Mama take it? Will she mess up? Will she upset Frankie?* I could see the doubt in his face.

With gritted teeth, I set out that day determined to be positive and calm during the appointment. The clinic is on the same busy thoroughfare as two irregularly shaped residential buildings recently featured in a powerful Canadian film called *Enemy* by the director Jean-Marc Vallée. These twin buildings, the Absolute Towers, which are beautiful in many respects, are sometimes called the Marilyn Munroe buildings due to their voluptuous curves and silhouettes and were allegedly inspired by her. They loomed ahead of me as I drove towards our destination. It felt like they were perversely mocking me, considering our task that day.

The clinic itself is outfitted like a high-end salon or spa in soft tones of cream, pink, and teal and adorned with graceful portraits of elegant ladies and flowers from a less challenging time, perhaps when one could grow old gracefully. One was a reproduction of a John Singer Sargent beauty — the 1892 portrait of *Lady Agnew of Lochnaw* — that I immediately recognized as I entered the salon. Each client I saw that day was *une femme d'un certain age* fighting the scourge of time. Begrudgingly, I admitted to myself that the staff was very friendly, welcoming Frankie with a great deal of enthusiasm and kindness — in a sort of cheerleader mode that set my teeth rattling with suppressed anger. I could not help noticing, disconcertedly, how many of the all-female staff had had work done on their faces. Many, if not all, had had, at the very least, Botox injections.

The first person we spoke to, to discuss the surgical procedure, the recovery, the post-surgery care, was a very pleasant woman a decade or so younger than me. She was well-dressed and had lovely, friendly manners. Frankie was blissed out, so excited, to finally be doing this. I couldn't help quietly tearing up during the discussion and the woman very kindly, and discreetly, handed me a tissue from a Kleenex box that she retrieved from the next room. Poor Frankie's face dropped in dismay when he saw me tearing up. I tried to hold it in, but I was struggling. At least I didn't burst out sobbing, which was my first impulse.

We awaited the surgeon and as the woman left the room she said very gently to me, "It's always harder at the beginning for the moms." After she left, I apologized to Frankie. He was disappointed in me but he told me it was okay, that he understood. But I had diminished his happiness that day and I knew it.

I had such rage in my heart against what fate had dealt us. Why did Frankie have to do this to himself to achieve a sense of normalcy, of being comfortable in his skin? I had asked him, practically begged him, many times to reconsider, to try and live within his own body. I told him he could dress as he liked, love whomever he loved, live as he wanted to live, but this did not assuage his sense of dysphoria. I realized now that it was cruel of me to ask him to do so. The anger I felt was unhealthy and my ill will was spreading towards these people in the clinic who were going to help Frankie achieve his goal.

The surgeon — kind, professional, fatherly in aspect — looked like he had partaken of some of the services offered. That made me inexplicably sad. What did it matter to me if someone used Botox? Or had a facelift? But it did make me a bit uncomfortable. I managed not to embarrass my child while the surgeon was in the room, but cannot now recall a single thing he said to us.

Afterwards, we were ushered into the office of the woman who handled the finances. We plunked down approximately eight thousand dollars on a credit card. As it was well beyond our credit limit, I had to make special arrangements with our bank to permit the transaction. I want to address that amount, because it was a bit of a circuitous route as to how we were able to afford the surgery.

We paid the amount, we exited the clinic, and as we did, with Frankie chattering and bobbing up and down excitedly as we left, I broke down sobbing along the corridor leading to the parking lot and continued crying all the way to the car and most of the way home. Frankie was upset with me, very upset, but he consoled me, putting his arm around my back and rubbing it. "It's okay, Mom, you needed to do this, you needed to be here," he said with resignation.

I tried to gather myself in the car. I apologized repeatedly for ruining this moment of liberation and joy for Frankie. I kept telling myself on the way home back to Toronto that my child was not happy in his body, had not been happy for a very long time; he had just adopted a brilliant disguise to fool us all.

THE SURGERY WAS BOOKED FOR April 20, 2015. We were up at five-thirty a.m. as we needed to be in the clinic in Mississauga by seven-thirty a.m. Frankie was quietly excited. Rob was upbeat. I was very quiet, I think almost resigned, during the drive. The surgery would take place at eight-thirty a.m. and would likely take two or three hours. We were to wait at the major shopping mall across the street until Frankie was awake and responsive after the surgery before we could bring him home.

Rob and I brought our computers and books and magazines to read. I bought us some breakfast at the Tim Hortons and we settled in. Rob was very calm, I was less so. Coffee followed coffee and we spoke little. I paced the mall. Then Rob paced the mall. It was just me, him, and all the little old men and ladies who frequent malls in the early morning hours. The wheels in my mind turned unceasingly. What had I agreed to? How would Frankie look after the surgery? Was it a mistake? Was I a compassionate mother or the biggest idiot on the planet to subject him to this? Would he change his mind one day? The question dogged me in the months preceding the operation and during the procedure that day. I feared, above all, irrevocable decisions. Name changes I could handle. Changes in Frankie's hairstyle, his clothing, the people he chose to date or befriend — but this would be a difficult thing to undo and I feared it.

At eleven-thirty a.m. we received the call that Frankie would be ready in about an hour for pickup. We thought we would surprise him with treats from the candy store. Rob suggested that we buy a baby blue cigar for Frankie to celebrate. It was wrapped in a peacock blue wrapper that read, *It's a boy!* I took a picture and posted it on Facebook without a message. Responses to my post started flooding in with well wishes from those in the know — as well as some puzzled questions that I couldn't bring myself to answer.

Just after noon Rob said, "It's time to go pick Frankie up." I took a portion of a Zopiclone tablet, a sleeping pill I take at night, to calm my nerves. Rob looked at me sympathetically, but said nothing. I didn't want to disgrace myself again at the clinic when we picked up Frankie. I was determined not to. I didn't.

Frankie was drowsy and very quiet when we met him, but in good spirits. We thanked the nurse who had wheeled him down to the parking lot in a wheelchair. We gave him his package of goodies, including the blue cigar. Through the haze of the medication he smiled gratefully and then Frankie peacefully dozed in the car beside me when we drove back to Toronto. And so began his new life with his new body.

# The Year I Came Out

❖

THERE WAS A POINT WHEN I felt I needed to be with other parents and relations of trans kids. A Parents Families & Friends of Lesbians & Gays (PFLAG) group met in a church basement just ten minutes east of our home. I had been circling around this group in my mind for months. I felt profoundly uncomfortable talking to people I was not close to about Frankie. Casual inquiries of "How's your daughter?" — clearly they had not heard the news — created spikes of anxiety and dread in me. The looks on their faces, as I explained our situation — confusion, anxiety, concern — was painful to me and for them, I suspect.

I could always tell who knew and who didn't know when I encountered someone in the neighbourhood or on the street. Those who knew had an expression that was equal parts anxiety, fear, and curiosity. This caused me to shut down emotionally. I couldn't deal with their anxiety and my own. How would it feel to be in a room where the admission that your son was trans would not raise eyebrows or elicit quizzical glances? I wanted to find out.

As I made my way into the meeting room, I was pleasantly greeted by the team leaders or facilitators of the group. I took my place beside a somewhat unhappy looking trans woman. My transphobia was kicking in. She was unfriendly and her awkward appearance was challenging my receptivity to her. I glanced about the room and was somewhat surprised by the average age of the participants. Many were considerably older — appearing to be possibly grandparents rather than parents — canes and walkers were visible everywhere. *What's going on here?* I wondered. Perhaps it was older relations who required the support and counselling. I saw few people in my age group with whom I could identify.

The group leader began asking newcomers what their stories were. When it came to me I started to waver and tear up as I spoke. The group leader was very knowledgeable and asked me astute questions about where Frankie was in his transition. She went about the room gently probing others about their gay or trans relations. She seemed to know them all. One mother proudly announced that she had a trans child, a bisexual child, and a pansexual child. She made it sound like they had been accepted to Julliard. I couldn't help thinking that, probably, it was inappropriate to display shame or reservations to strangers — but to display pride? Was there a source of pride in proclaiming your child's gender and/or sexual identity? Should we perceive it as an accomplishment of some sort?

A woman, who was a friend to a parent at the meeting, peppered the crowd and the group leader with trans 101 questions, asking for definitions and explanations of terms and assiduously writing down information in a notebook. She dominated the discussion. This irked me — mind you, I was nervous and uncomfortable. Was this an info session for those curious about LGBTQ issues or a support group for relations? Unsettled, I did not speak for the remainder of the meeting. The group was not unfriendly, it was quite the opposite, but they seemed reluctant to speak up. Perhaps they had already had their public moments of angst and had settled comfortably into a mild acceptance.

I was still full of fear and confusion, sometimes even rage. I was not at peace with my destiny as the mother of a trans child. I could not see past what Frankie's transition meant to me, what it said about me. I wasn't thinking of Frankie and Frankie alone. I was not there yet. I hoped to be one day, but clearly I had not reached this stage of acceptance. I wanted a forum in which I could vent my frustration. This venue was far too genteel for me, too accepting, despite their kindness. When I left that night I knew I had not found my tribe. I had yet to find it. But it had been difficult to confess to Frankie how alone I felt, how isolated and afraid.

I BEGAN TO SEE DR. B, a therapist, semi-regularly. She was refreshingly direct and bore a strong physical resemblance to Sarah Jessica Parker — long pretty blond hair, very fit, fashionable, and chic. Even though she was younger than me, she had a very soothing Jewish mother vibe — tough but compassionate. Wise but open to my contrarian thoughts. When I was being a jerk, she could be very direct in her advice. She also reassured me when I was on the right track as a mom and praised me often when she thought I handled difficult situations effectively.

One time she said to me after a very emotional session, "I really don't know why you are not in here every week. You do have insurance benefits to cover the sessions, right?"

"Yes."

"But why are you not here more often then?" she asked kindly.

How could I explain this? It felt unseemly to whine about this situation. Although, the reader may ask rightly, what am I doing by writing this memoir? Is the honesty a form of whining? I felt like I should have a grip on this. It had been three years since Frankie came out; when would I be able to deal with this issue without the drama and the sorrow? No crying, no melancholy, just living a normal life and proceeding normally with all that life holds for me.


TWENTY-THIRTEEN WAS THE YEAR I came out as a person who feared and misunderstood gender identity and sexual orientation. Who feared the future and her responsibility to her child. Who raged against her fate. Who slumped into a depression at times at the thought of what lay ahead. A person masquerading as a compassionate person, masquerading as a brave mother, masquerading as a whole person, when I knew I had been broken into a million pieces.

That year my heart shrivelled to a pea. That year my heart grew, Grinch-like, three sizes bigger. That year I vowed I would destroy anyone for my child if he was harmed. That year I tested the boundaries of my marriage. That year I was prepared to lose my entire extended family if it chose to forsake my child. That year I knew I would survive if only to ensure that my child would thrive.

I ran the full gamut of emotions. Most days. Emotions raged and washed over me, engulfed me, threatened to overwhelm me. On most days, if a friend or family member asked how I was doing, I would answer "Good!" The truth was more complicated — somewhere between happy and miserable. I was happy when my child was happy — doing well at school, succeeding in his work, in his relationships and with his emotional and physical health. I was sometimes miserable when things were not going well for him, when his health was in jeopardy, if he faced discrimination or hostility as a trans person, or if people were intransigent in referring to him with male pronouns.

But frankly, some days, I felt a bit saddened when I thought about Frankie's fate. I have always hated the "Why me?" question that beleaguered people often ask when they are met with disappointment, large or small; but I do think it, if not openly express it. The self-pity in that question is endlessly annoying and self-involved. Why not you? Why not me? Why should it be someone else who suffers these anxieties and travails?

Much of the anxiety I felt was the fear that my child would always struggle because he decided to live an open and honest life. That would be his burden as well as ours. So it was an endless emotional seesaw between relief that he is sorting his life out and sadness that a loved one struggles. I was immensely proud of the person Frankie was becoming as a young adult: compassionate, loyal, socially aware, intellectually curious, artistically and musically talented, affectionate, and charming.

When I first began to write down my thoughts, I wondered if I had made a misstep — my lack of knowledge about the transgender experience had frightened me into assuming that I — and we as parents — had encouraged my child down a certain path. I understand more fully now that we had nothing to do with creating Frankie's gender identity but we did have a bit to do with creating a welcoming, loving environment in which he could come out.

I learned many things over the last several years.

Trans does not equal gay and trans people don't appreciate it when these terms are used interchangeably.

I see, no I feel, the inquisitive looks, the unanswered questions from those around us at times. *How could you let him do this? How can you support this?* I think some people feel they could not take this on or, more disturbingly, they would not let it happen. We are not "letting" Frankie be trans. Frankie is, however, choosing to be open about what he feels, who he is. We are not permitting Frankie to get "everything he wants" from us by being trans. He is not "getting away" with anything.

My hope is that family and friends will try to avoid repeatedly telling us we're great, that our child is lucky to have us. It really is more about Frankie's courage. I understand that they want to offer support but as most parents will tell you — they feel they have no option but to support the most important and vulnerable people in their lives. The *child* is brave, strong; the *child* has tremendous guts to proceed like this openly.

I'd like sympathetic people to avoid asking about the physical specifics of Frankie's transition. That's his personal business. That's our personal business. I know people are curious. I would be, too. But it's not Frankie's obligation to share this information.

# On Chaz, On Caitlyn

❖

I FEEL THAT WE CAN'T talk about being transgender without addressing the issue of the most well-known, highly publicized trans man and trans woman currently on the planet — Chaz Bono and Caitlyn Jenner. Like many others who felt they had no connection or emotional investment in treating these persons with respect, I was cheerfully and blissfully dismissive of their trials and tribulations in the media.

I didn't understand what I was witnessing on this very public stage when Chaz Bono transitioned from female to male between 2008 and 2010. I was somewhat alarmed by the transition at some point, and, perhaps, mightily relieved I did not have to deal with this issue as a mother. As they say, pride comes before the fall. At best, I was condescendingly sympathetic at publicly witnessing his evolution from adorable little girl, daughter of the singing duo Sonny and Cher, to out lesbian and LGBTQ activist as a young adult, to trans man and transgender advocate. Now, because this hits so close to home, I am completely mortified by the manner in which he is sometimes referred to in the media. If it is not outright hostility, then it's a quietly snickering attitude.

Flash forward to Caitlyn Jenner's transition in the spring and summer of 2015 and I could see it from a very different perspective as a mother of a trans child. Now, because I was so close to the situation with my own child, I could no longer be blasé or amused at what I see. Whether it was the paparazzi provoking Jenner before she outed herself as trans or seeing images of a Caitlyn Jenner Halloween costume for men posted online, or pointless and insulting criticism of her high femme style as a woman — now it was personal. And infuriating.

Is it really anyone's concern if Jenner likes pretty clothes and makeup? Does it set back the cause of transgender people if she favours manicures and weaves? I can't help thinking that even the progressive people who purport to be feminists and trans-positive are anti-femme when they criticize her style as if things that are feminine — and I include even the supremely artificially feminine — are inferior, shallow, less than human. It's as if the embracing of masculine style or an androgynous style is a superior political and personal stance. If femininity is a social construct, it's my construct to employ or destroy and no amount of finger wagging likely will dissuade someone who chooses to embrace it.

If you knew someone who went through this transition, if you knew how hard it is to come out to the people who love you the most, if you saw how difficult it was to do the most basic things — purchase clothes, find a bathroom, change your name, feel comfortable in your own skin — you might have second thoughts before you started snickering about it or making jokes. It's been a long, difficult journey in a very public forum for both of them — whether you think they have been successful at it or not — and it's their journey to make. If anything, I have felt intense empathy for Bono's mother, Cher, now in her seventies, who sometimes has expressed sorrow, confusion, and resistance to Chaz's decision to transition.

My child has said to us on more than one occasion, "If I had choice, I would not go through this." He has often expressed a wish that things were not so difficult for him. But this feeling almost always centres on trying to battle the fear and discomfort that other people feel towards the transition. I would say that Frankie is comfortable in his decision to transition, but dealing with other people's fears and insecurities is another matter. It is awkward and uncomfortable, conforming to new ideas, considering revolutionary ways of thinking about gender, sexual orientation, gender roles, what it means to be masculine, what it means to be feminine. Frankie is a pioneer in this area, in the vanguard of a new way of being. It may be discomfiting to some, but it is a brave, new world now and I, we, must adjust.

It's not a choice about a lifestyle. Now I finally understand why some gay people are so dismayed by the use of the term "gay lifestyle," as if it's some sort of fashionable attire you've acquired for a season. Coming out, transitioning, is an honest, brave embracing of being true to one's inner self. It's not a question of wanting to be something else, it's a question of needing to be something else — to have the external correspond with the internal and to have it validated by the people you care about, as well as those you don't.

# Caged

❖

SOMETHING PRETTY AMAZING HAPPENED IN Frankie's last year
of high school regarding his artwork. He was invited by the
Magenta Foundation, at the recommendation of his art teachers
at his high school, to participate in the Fast Forward Incubator
Program Art Exhibit at Twist Gallery in September 2014. The
Foundation is a non-profit, charitable arts publishing house
created to organize promotional opportunities for artists, in
an international context, through circulated exhibitions and
publications. The exhibit was sponsored by TD Bank. Approximately forty or fifty students from two prominent arts high
schools were invited to create self-portraits using a variety
of media.

Rob was initially nervous as Frankie seemed so lacka-
daisical about finishing the project, which would need to be
completed before school ended in June — a date that was
approaching rapidly. Perhaps Frankie was being protective
about the subject matter — he did not tell me in advance
what the image would consist of, although his dad knew.

Frankie chose the medium of photography and asked his dad
to help him shoot it in his room using one white wall as a
backdrop. He was secretive about the photograph and I soon
learned why.

In the photograph, Frankie is naked, seated, and shot from
behind and the image starts just above his hips with his two
hands poised along his back. You see red claw marks on the
back and the hands are raised in such a way that they suggest
torment or violence. The piece is titled *Caged*. Clearly, the
viewer can see that the person he seeks to be is trapped inside
this body.

The image saddened me immensely, but I was heartened
and proud too. I was proud of his artistic talent and his ability
to express his pain in art. I was proud of the fact that he is
determined to be honest about the challenges of his life. It's
beautiful in its composition, sincere, and powerful. It reflects
perfectly his intense desire to transition.

When we went to the reception in honour of the students — a catered, elegant affair in the gallery with hundreds
of people attending — I was delighted to see someone had
bid on it at the silent auction. "Your first sale!" I squealed in
delight, but Frankie quietly reminded me that, actually, it
was his second. Frankie had also entered a piece in an exhibit
when he was receiving counselling at Delisle Youth Services
years ago. That, too, had sold.

We have photos of Frankie standing in front of the art,
looking sheepish but proud. Hell, that's the way I feel when I
look at it too.

# Back to School (or Not)

✦

THE FIRST YEAR OF UNIVERSITY for Frankie was unexpectedly tumultuous. I had hoped, after a successful, if challenging, last year of high school that we had surmounted a major hurdle and Frankie had learned to manage the demands of school and living his life. Frankie had made the honour roll, won an award for his art, participated in the yearbook, and managed to be in school most days. The school he had set his heart on was prestigious, well-respected, and a close thirty-minute streetcar ride away. But the year proved to be difficult.

Frankie found the program unexpectedly hard. He thought his classmates unfriendly, the curriculum demanding, some teachers indifferent and uninspiring. He was bored and unmotivated. He took five courses, then dropped down to three courses the first term; the following February, he couldn't keep up. He felt his medication was no longer working as well as it had. Eventually, we switched to another prescription with a moderate, beneficial change. The end of the school year seemed to help his state of mind. It alleviated some of

the pressure on him. But as the summer after the school year
ended we saw the strain of Frankie's anxieties peak again. It
was obvious he was dreading school, even with a suggested
reduced course load. He was slipping into old patterns of
depression and social anxiety, much like the first years when
his depression surfaced at the age of twelve.

Exhaustion. Inability to sleep. Lethargy. Depression. Social
anxiety. Loss of enthusiasm and lack of interest in everything.
Unwillingness to attend family or social functions. His bedroom was a chaotic mess of discarded clothes, used dishes,
loose papers and change, bottles, and unread books in a state
of disarray. We had an agreement that he could do as he
liked in his room as long as he was orderly in the rest of the
house. But this had reached a new stage of disorder. When we
talked about his depression he asked, "Haven't you noticed,
Mom, how bad my room is?" Even in his depressed state, he
realized that the chaos of the room was representative of an
unhappy, disorganized mind — the chaos without, mirroring
the chaos within.

In October, one month into the second year of university, Frankie said he wanted to talk to us both about attending
school. He wanted to take a break. He promised he would
return in a year. Privately, Rob had been suggesting to me
that it would be better for Frankie if he left school briefly.
I was resistant initially, adamant that he remain, even on a
part-time basis. My fear was that without school or a job or
any kind of structure he would sink even further into lethargy
and despair.

I will admit I was heartbroken at the thought of him not

being in school. I never expected that my child would dislike school, detest it even. I had mostly enjoyed school from the moment I set foot in kindergarten at Holy Name of Jesus grade school in my working-class neighbourhood. Even though school was sometimes harsh — I remember bare-ass spankings the first year and a nun with a predilection for strapping unruly children who had transgressed some minor rule — school was a haven for me. I was no longer a second-class citizen as I sometimes felt I was treated at home, where, as a girl, I was required to make my younger brother's bed, perform household chores, and obey my parents and the adults in my life unconditionally. No one at school ever suggested I wasn't smart enough to attend law school or that I should perhaps consider an alternative white-collar job as a bank teller — as one relation suggested with what I can only assume was kindly intent or a misguided sense of my presumed place in the world.

At home, reading was frowned upon if it was not speci- fically for a school assignment or an exam. A book in hand meant too much leisure time. At eighteen, probably in the midst of a fairly high-functioning depression, after a traumatic relationship had abruptly ended, I began to read voraciously — as if to submerge myself for protection from the outside world. I think I thought, subconsciously, that if I was reading I didn't have to interact with anyone. This was not seen as a useful enterprise at home. Why read when there was cleaning to be done? Indeed, why? I expected, perhaps unrealistically, that school and reading would be as important to Frankie as they were to me. That they weren't saddened and puzzled me.

But my feelings were more complicated than disappointment in him. I felt I was failing as a mother. I felt I couldn't keep him healthy and happy. I couldn't keep him engaged in the world. I couldn't keep him in school. If I had failed in these crucial areas, had I not also failed as a mother?

I was trying hard to shake myself out of my disappointment and self-pity because Frankie, of all those closest to me, was the most astute at determining how I was feeling and I didn't want my negative feelings to impact his already low mood even further.

I tried to understand Frankie's leaving school by examining the ways I had disappointed my own mother. I left home at nineteen to live on my own and attend university in a city forty miles from Hamilton. I left her, a relatively young widow in her early forties, to manage a small, family owned business on her own with the aid of my teenage brother. I felt my family situation was intolerable and I was beyond miserable at home. But, at that time and with my family, it was still considered unacceptable to leave the family home as an unmarried woman. One cousin advised me that it was my moral obligation to remain with my mother until I married or she died, whichever came first, both immensely unappealing options to my nineteen-year-old ears.

I married outside of my culture, outside of my ethnic group and race. Although that was not my perception. And although my mother has come to love Rob a great deal, her first reaction was to be unhappy and dissatisfied when she met him, casting visual daggers when they met at my university graduation ceremony — as his own mother did to me at the same ceremony. I chose a liberal arts education, graduated during a recession, and floated rootlessly for a number of years before finally landing in a corporate environment that eventually paid well and offered numerous perks, but it was a career that did not suit me and I eventually abandoned it.

My path has always been inexplicable to my mother and she fought or challenged me at every juncture when I deviated from the life she envisioned. She had contemplated a certain type of life for me. I refused to adhere to it, very aggressively pursuing an alternative path. She found me obstinate and selfish, lazy and uncooperative. My relations did as well when I lit out for the big bad city of Toronto. I felt I had no advocate and no protection from their censure, and they could not understand that I had no desire to marry a local boy, attend the university in my hometown so that I wouldn't have to leave my family and settle into a secure, middle class existence in the bosom of my familial relations.

In my opposition to Frankie's desire, wasn't I doing the same to him? I wanted him to excel academically, to be literate and university educated like his father and me. But what if this was not his path? He is a bright but not academically inclined kid. He had literally begged for a year off before he started, sensing possible disaster, but we had pushed him into entering his first year of university, which he hated and resented.

A few months after he left school, and for no specific reason, I asked him if he ever thought of suicide in his darkest moments.

"Yes, I have," he answered reluctantly.

"When was the last time?" I asked.

"Before I started school the second year."

That's how much he hated it. This was a frightening blow to me. Now, at this juncture in his life, I had to ask myself what was more important — my pride and vision for his future or his happiness and mental health?

I am happy to report that Frankie has decided to return to university part-time, possibly changing his discipline. He is anxious to start a new path, learning and expanding intellectually, and Rob and I are happy to support him in any academic venture he pursues.

# On the Job

✦

ROB AND I AGREED THAT Frankie should be working during his year off from school, but I was nervous at the prospect. Jobs for trans kids can be notoriously difficult to find and keep. Retailers, the principal employers of teenagers, can be a bit ruthless in exploiting them and disrespecting their rights.

In the first position Frankie actively pursued while in high school, he was hired by a national frozen yogurt franchise. He actually sought this franchise out and decided it would be a good place to work. The franchise owner was young, confident, and clearly inexperienced, lacking that crucial filter when dealing with kids, specifically young women entering the workforce for the first time. He told the staff that he only hired good looking people and speculated aloud that he wanted to be careful how many Asians he hired for his location as it was based in an area that catered to Greek cuisine and a mostly white clientele. He himself was Asian. These pronouncements were met with confusion and embarrassment by Frankie. How should he react to these remarks? Did these statements cross the line and, if so, what could he do in this situation? It was difficult for him to determine.

The owner also had an alarming habit of hitting on the underage girls. He seemed to favour them by granting privileges and more shifts than some of the other staff. Frankie, as a trans boy, appeared to be at a disadvantage. When Frankie made small errors his shifts were reduced to nothing. This increased his nervousness and hence the potential to mess up. Demoralized and confused as to why he had fallen out of favour, he quit after a few months.

When Frankie started university he worked part-time in a bookstore on campus. It was a time when his gender might have been perceived as ambiguous. A few of the sales clerks with whom he worked couldn't seem to grasp the use of male pronouns. But I was proud of how Frankie handled the situation. He wrote each of them personally explaining that he was trans and respectfully requested that they employ male pronouns. Some, apparently, could not. Despite liking the manager very much and lacking a significant number of shifts, Frankie left that position.

During the summer, after the first school year at university ended, Frankie got another job working in the kitchen of a sandwich shop on a trendy strip of Queen West. With an all-Asian staff, including the manager, initially Frankie felt very comfortable. I joked that he had found his people. However, one error on the production line during a shift left him without shifts for two weeks. When I pressed Frankie to be more aggressive with the manager in requesting more shifts, he was hesitant. I knew there was something else behind his reticence.

He had not been paid yet because he had not brought in his SIN card. It turned out he was afraid his manager would see his old birth name on the card — a very feminine name that we had not changed over yet — and would then know Frankie was trans.

When Frankie finally received shifts again he was helpfully told by a coworker that his error had resulted in his being penalized with no shifts. He was told other things as well: the managers spied on the employees while they prepared the food and Frankie's coworkers had been gossiping about him, something Frankie had suspected for a while but was unable to prove as the chatter was not in English. Shortly afterwards, Frankie quit.

It's possible these employers would be difficult with anyone, particularly vulnerable young people, not just a trans kid. However, the problem lies in the anxiety for trans teens that they are being penalized for being trans: "Your looks are off." "You're not passing." People are uneasy with them as they transition; and the trans kids get the vibe they are being gossiped about.

Frankie's plan to find work in lieu of school was a discouraging one for me based on his brief experiences in these scenarios. I didn't want to be one of those overly demanding parents who urge their kids with bromides like: "I didn't raise a quitter!" but I sure felt like one. Many of us have difficult bosses and unfriendly coworkers. We feel disconnected from the work and the workforce. But trans kids have special obstacles.

# Welcome to My Fortress

✦

I WAS NOT SHOCKED OR dismayed when Katie Couric asked
Laverne Cox, an actor and transgender woman, about her
genitals during a television interview in 2014. I admit I
was curious — I wanted to know as well. Now, in light of
my son's transition, I am horrified by this rude inquiry and
my own intrusive curiosity. What right do I have to this
information about others?

I want to raise an issue that I dislike talking about
intensely: cis gender privilege. Many an argument has raged
in our house about cis privilege, my own perceived privilege as a cis person, and that of my cis brethren. Simply
put, cis people have the luxury of not only controlling the
political system, the medical establishment, the legal structure and the rules of society — basically all facets of day to
day life which may either enhance or destroy the happiness
of trans people.

I dislike the term, because in disagreements with my
son it tends to destroy dialogue, to destroy communication.

But it does exist and it inhibits the true understanding of persons that we, as cis, perceive to be unlike ourselves.

It might be suggested that the interlocutor, in this case a seasoned journalist, was merely trying to understand for herself and her viewers what it is to be trans. But does that extend to the particulars of her guest's genitalia? Understanding the enormity of that violation is difficult, if not impossible, until cis privilege hits you right in the face.

SOMEHOW I KNEW THAT THIS lunch would not go well. A casual acquaintance had been dogging me for months, asking for a lunch meeting; she had a request in mind that I might be able to help her with, with regards to her literary career, and I was reluctant to oblige. She often veered from fawning attention to hostility within minutes — without rhyme or reason. I somewhat expected more of the same during our lunch at this small Italian café I sometimes frequent near my place of work. I was unsure if she was aware of Frankie's transition, even though she knew I was writing some sort of a personal memoir. Oh, she knew. And she was quick off the mark in getting more information about it.

"How much did your son's surgery cost?" she asked before the first entrée arrived.

"That's a little personal, don't you think?" I said as pleasantly as my surprise would allow. I was determined to shut down the conversation. Immediately.

"Is that what you would say to a journalist who asked you about your book?" she said in an aggressive tone. She held up a saltshaker as if it was a microphone and pointed it towards me as if I was being interviewed.

"I might," I said, with only the tiniest edge in my voice, trying to suppress my anger.

"Well, won't it be in your book?"

"It might," I said again. "I don't know. Maybe."

"Don't you think it would help the parents of other trans kids to know the cost?"

"Yes, probably ..."

I tried to explain. I did not want to open up this issue for that ever-present and outraged taxpayer who doesn't believe that they should help to allay the costs of surgery for trans people. The surgery had not been billed through OHIP — we, with the assistance of concerned friends and family, had paid for it. But if it was a heart defect or a broken leg — no one would have the gall to suggest that we shouldn't try to heal someone or alleviate their pain. She nodded with seeming understanding. Or so I thought.

The food came. I glanced at our waitress gratefully and paid an inordinate amount of attention to my chicken panini, but to no avail. With despair I saw that she was trying to resume the conversation. A woman at the table beside me had a coughing fit. I ran to the counter and got her a glass of water. She accepted it gratefully.

When my lunch mate resumed her inquiry, I finally said in an exasperated tone, "Yes, I see your point ... but why do you want to have this information?"

She seemed stymied.

"Oh, I just thought because Caitlyn Jenner and the Kardashians are always talking about their plastic surgery, you would be open to discussing it."

"Look," I said, "would you ask the woman beside us if those were her real breasts and how much they cost?" I think I hit a nerve then and finally managed to turn her off.

And just so I understood this in my own mind: Because Caitlyn Jenner, a trans woman, is the stepparent of the Kardashian brood and has been open about her transition and various surgeries, I should be open about whether my son has had surgery and how much it cost? Has my child, by virtue of this transition, opened himself up to this relentless examination of his actions and life because he is trans? Some trans people have surgery; some trans people do not. Some trans men have top and bottom surgery. Some only have top surgery. Some do absolutely nothing to their bodies surgically.

Who should control the trans body? In the same manner that people who are not black have terrorized, owned, abused, and sold the black body and in the same manner that we have objectified, sexualized, and tried to control the female body, those who hold the reins of power, or benefit from reins of power, believe they are entitled to control, examine, judge, vilify the trans body.

I don't think that cis people understand fully that the trans body does not belong to them. Nor does it belong to me despite my intimate connection to a trans person. Relinquish that expectation of control. Suppress curiosity and intrusive inquiry. Try to remember that we are dealing with human beings experiencing one of the most profound self-revelations about themselves and unprecedented changes to their bodies. We should respect that.

Sometimes I see my home, my life, my role, as a fortress with Frankie at the centre and me and Rob on the barricades keeping the barbarians at bay, protecting him. "You shall not pass," I sometimes mutter through clenched teeth. In a manner, I am grateful for these unpleasant interactions. It reminds me of what I am fighting for and for whom.

# One of Our Own

✦

I WAS SHOCKED, AND RELIEVED, at how accepting our families were, for the most part. When my brother Charlie said to my mother that I was afraid she couldn't accept Frankie, my mother indignantly replied, "Why? Isn't Frankie one of our own?" Yes, he is. He is one of our own.

No more mysterious headaches, stomach aches, chest pains, pains in the foot. He certainly has his blue days, but they are fewer and fewer now. He is lighter, happier, more joyous. Rob says he is back to the old Frankie.

It is not all sunshine and roses for the three of us. Recently Rob and I were in the car together and a song came on that was so melancholic and poignant, it spoke to us regarding rising up to the challenge of great adversities. The song always reminds both of us of the trials of Frankie's young life and at that moment Rob broke down crying. I knew he was thinking of Frankie. He said, "I love him so much. I never want to leave him. I never want to go." He spoke of the inevitable, the unnameable, the thing that haunted us when we thought of the future. "Yes," I said, "I know." We will always be here for him, I thought. We will never desert him.

Here is a secret for the parents of transgender, children: whoever your child is before the transition, she or he will remain the same afterwards emotionally and psychologically, if not physically. If he was funny, loving, intellectually curious, artistic, he will stay that way. I know our child did.

The essence of the person you loved remains; it doesn't disappear. Ever.

# The Soul of This Room

✦

AT THE END OF DECEMBER 2015, Frankie decided that he would move into the self-contained apartment in the basement of our house. It was my idea initially, but eventually he and his father enthusiastically embraced it. Frankie would pay a modest rent from his part-time job and live a somewhat separate existence from his parents with his girlfriend for the first time in his young life. He was nervous at the prospect but the unit was recently vacated by a tenant and it would allow for autonomy, personal responsibility for rent and other expenses, having to do one's own laundry and buy groceries, cooking one's own meals, and keeping the apartment reasonably orderly. It would be a good beginning for a young trans boy who is coming out. And he would be close by if he needed us.

When Frankie moved out, just before New Year's Eve, it gave me a chance to clean up his bedroom which had been virtually untouched by parental hands in years. Ever the neurotic mother, I would occasionally ask to have it cleaned up but was always unceremoniously shut down with the observation that it was his space to do with what he wanted. Point taken.

The bedroom has built-in floor-to-ceiling white book-shelves on the west side of the room, where Rob and I have stored most of our books, CDs, and VHS tapes, as well as various other mementos. There is a large window facing the door with a panel of stained glass at the top that illuminates the room on sunny days and looks onto the street. It has its original wooden floors and a large closet that still houses Frankie's clothes, my wedding dress, and all of Frankie's old Halloween costumes, too precious to throw out or donate.

Now as I processed what I would have to clean up, I was looking at a melange of books and also loose papers, completed and uncompleted artwork by Frankie, bric-a-brac, forgotten piles of change, tiny blunt pencils, some of Frankie's health and beauty products, bits of old toys, unused yellowing envelopes left over from Rob's father's printing business, unused gift cards presented to Frankie, dozens of guitar picks, greeting cards for various occasions exchanged between the three of us, our old record albums, Rob's 45s and his dad's old 78 rpm records, several pieces of Frankie's earrings, and a tiny array of Pokémon figures.

I was daunted by my task to clear up the room and move my desk into it so that I might have my own space to write again. Currently, my desk was shoved in a corner of our bed-room and, as nice a space as it was, I found it hard to work there. In Frankie's room it was as if I was an archeologist exploring the various layers of our shared lives — probing the soul of this room, the soul of my child, of my expectations of my child. Every discovery undid me a little. I had forgotten how much of Frankie's complex history was stored here.

On the left side of the bookshelves, where most of my books were, was a pantheon of my personal female heroes — their works and biographies — women who inspired me, who I aspired to be, whom I wanted my child to emulate as she grew into a young woman.

*Susan Sontag, Simone de Beauvoir, the poet and novelist Louise Colet (once Flaubert's mistress), Louis Bryant, Germaine Greer, Edna St. Vincent Millay, Sylvia Plath.*

Allow me the privilege of sometimes referring to Frankie as "she" when I speak of the time before he came out as trans. I found Frankie's first sippy cup — blue-topped and adorned with two kittens. What was that doing here, wedged between books? A small pink satin heart with edges embroidered in ivory lace, which I had placed in Frankie's cradle when she was born. A Beatrix Potter calendar from the year after she was born. I had aspirations to paint some Potter figures on the wall of Frankie's first bedroom. Something I never did. Should I have thrown it out? No, I left it aside. Several stuffed toys were wedged in between the books — a small lion we named Simba during our first major holiday in the Caribbean. I threw him in the laundry once and he came back with an afro much to Frankie's chagrin. A fluffy lamb I bought a few years ago, an electric-blue kitten, provenance unknown. Photos of Frankie with his two best friends whom he has known since he was four.

*Frida Kahlo, Clara Bow, bandit queen Phoolan Devi, Sylvia Beach,*

*Patti Smith, Molly Haskell, Tilly Olsen, Pauline Kael, Djuna Barnes, Vita Sackville-West, Susan Faludi.*

VHS tapes of every Disney film Frankie loved, some made from bootleg copies that Frankie's uncle Kevin (Rob's cousin who passed away suddenly several years ago) made for him. The tiny Pokémon figures I noticed earlier, no higher than a thumbnail, posed along a lower shelf. I placed them in a plastic bag with other small items that he might want to keep. A brightly painted blue-and-red clay impression of Frankie's toddler hand that had cracked in half. Some eight-by-ten colour photos of Frankie and his father cavorting in a lake, taken at a cottage we rented one summer with Rob's siblings. Frankie looked about eight. *Don't tell me that kid was not happy*, I pled to myself, taking in the look of joy on Frankie's face as she was pulled along in an inflatable beach toy by her father.

*Italian journalist Oriana Fallaci, Man Ray's favourite model Kiki de Montparnasse (Alice Prin), Yoko Ono, Katherine Mansfield, Louise Brooks, Angela Davis.*

Then I stumbled upon some photos in a bland manila envelope, taken of Frankie in the daycare on the day when they made the unfortunate decision to dress the little girls up in princess costumes and put wreaths of flowers in their hair. When I came to pick up Frankie that day, I experienced a mild feeling of discomfort when they told me how they had spent the afternoon. The daycare workers told me excitedly that Frankie looked beautiful in the photos. I couldn't picture Frankie in a fairy costume, flowers in her hair, let down from her tight dark braids. I was right. The pictures, when we saw them, were disturbing in light of what we now know. Frankie looked uneasy even though she was smiling. Rob asked me then how did they make our kid, whom we think is so photogenic, look so uncomfortable in these photos? Now we know. When I showed them to Rob, he urged me to throw them out. He disliked them intensely, too, but I couldn't do that; I couldn't destroy any picture of Frankie's. I just couldn't, although I knew that I would never show them to Frankie, or anyone else, ever again.

*Harper Lee, Katharine Hepburn, Virginia Woolf, Azar Nafisi, Camille Paglia, Mitford sisters — except the one who married the British fascist and the one in love with Hitler.*

There were CD compilations of music that Rob made for Frankie of the music of many of the pop teen princesses from when she was a tween, never to be played again. Guitar picks by the score in various colours and images on a number of shelves and sheet music from the guitar lessons Frankie often refused to go to because she was so exhausted or anxious or unhappy then. A row of hardcover YA books from the ubiquitous *Twilight* to more mature fare recently acquired, but largely unread, it appeared. Numerous blank journals, at least a half dozen, awaiting new adventures and dreams. Exercise books with little in them, barely started, then abandoned also. A framed photo of Rob and me when we first met in our twenties in a heart-shaped frame. One of us when we married on the shore of Lake Ontario in a white, fairy-like gazebo, surrounded by family and friends.

*Edith Wharton, Joyce Carol Oates, Australian designer Florence Broadhurst, Mary Wollstonecraft and daughter Mary Shelley, Adrienne Rich, Jane Austen, Anais Nin.*

The photo we posted on the adoption website when we were hoping to have a second child. The photo of the extended family when we went to the Dominican Republic and Frankie made that fateful observation to himself that he was not who he thought he was. Various straps, cords, and plugs for pieces of cellphones and technology, now long discarded. A yellowed envelope of dried blood-red and golden rose petals that his ex-girlfriend, Julia, never received. An unopened box of men's cologne I gave Frankie the Christmas after he came out. Haphazard piles of graphic design and photography textbooks from Frankie's first year of university — pristine, barely used, worth hundreds of dollars. Notes from lectures and tutorials in Frankie's neat, graceful script. This made me both sorrowful and angry. It was so wasteful and futile — like trying to press a square peg in a round hole and then getting angry at the square peg for its impertinence.

*Joan Didion, nineteenth century Sicilian writer Maria Messina, firebrand feminist Betty Friedan, Rebecca Solnit, painter Vanessa Bell, Carson McCullers, Roxane Gay.*

As I neared the last shelf, cleaning and rearranging — setting aside things for Frankie to examine, things to throw out, things to donate, things to reuse — I examined my shelves of heroes and role models and started to think of the weight of my expectations on Frankie to be a certain sort of child, a certain sort of young woman, to be a certain type of person: intellectual, educated, creative, politically aware, brave, bold, revolutionary. What child could withstand that weight? That level of expectation?

"Kill your darlings," they say in writing classes. Rid yourself of all that you hold sacred for the sake of improving your writing. I think now, in a similar vein, discard your heroes. Let them go. Frankie is my role model now, he is my hero. He is the person that I most respect and whose bravery I wish to emulate.

# One Last Thing

✦

ONE OF FRANKIE'S CLOSEST FRIENDS, Pablo, a boy he considered to be a sort of surrogate brother, passed away unexpectedly. We are very close to the parents of this boy and the whole family; these are people we have known for almost twenty years. We have vacationed with them, had many birthday dinners together, celebrated holidays, and were at one time neighbours on our old street in Riverdale. I can't quite believe he is gone. We were all absolutely stunned. The death was completely unexpected and the results of the autopsy were inconclusive but suggested an undiagnosed heart ailment. In this case, he went to sleep one night and never woke up.

This eighteen-year-old-boy, Pablo, was one of two twins, the eldest of the two. We used to joke, as he was born a few minutes before his brother, that he was therefore the oldest child of the trio. I would sometimes jokingly task him with keeping the other two in line. When I went to visit my friends the day after that fateful discovery, the father of the boy immediately showed me a picture of the three kids sitting on the lawn of our old row house. The kids were perhaps three or four and sitting in a pile of leaves with beatific looks on their faces and covered by golden, brown, and bright red leaves. I felt a tightening in my chest when I saw that photo. One child would die before his nineteenth birthday. One child, we would learn, was trans. One would experience the loss of the death of his twin. Who could have foretold what those children would one day experience? We all agreed it was our favourite of the many photos we had of the three children over the last eighteen years.

When a bit younger, Frankie would tease Pablo, saying that if they had not married by forty that Frankie would marry him. From what I remember, Pablo never completely agreed to this proposal, but so be it.

That Sunday morning, when we learned of his death, I clung to Frankie while we told him this terrible news. Later I implored him, "Don't do anything dangerous," as I did not know the cause of Pablo's death at that time. I couldn't bear the thought of anything happening to him. But what did that mean? Don't live? Don't experiment? Don't be human?

In light of this news, I realized how ridiculous I was being about the transition — I had a healthy, beautiful, talented, kind-hearted, moderately happy child. Why was I wishing for something more? It seemed the height of greed and folly.

# Finishing the Unfinished Dollhouse

❖

OVER THE CHRISTMAS HOLIDAYS RECENTLY, we were listening to an old Disney tune — you'd recognize it immediately if I mentioned its name. Its theme is a common, if well-loved, trope. There is a beautiful princess, a poor boy with aspirations, and a meddlesome blue genie, and it's set in an exotic location. When Frankie was a toddler, literally still sitting in a car seat, I was compelled to play the soundtrack over and over to and from any given destination. It often drove me to distraction then, but Frankie was adamant about hearing it. Repeatedly. The main song, a beautiful one, admittedly, was about the young princess, who had led a confined and stultifying life, discovering a "whole new world." Without overstating this, it struck me that this little princess, too, had had her whole life planned out for her by her parents, and was rejecting it.

As Rob played it for me again recently, the song resonated in a new way. It is indeed a whole new world for Frankie — wondrous, exciting, challenging — down a path that is unexpected and potentially fraught with danger. I thought to myself that what the song may have meant to that beautiful baby was not what it means for Frankie now. And so, the day before Christmas, the tears came once again.

MY HAPPINESS AND SENSE OF relief regarding the ongoing resolution of Frankie's gender identity is mixed with melancholy. I loved being the mother of a daughter. Now I must resolve to be the loving mother of a son. I want my child to be happy, but I am sometimes uneasy at his hard and difficult choices — as my own mother often was with mine.

I hoped for grandchildren, which may or may not happen. Suddenly, it is very important to me in a way it was not a few years ago. If it does happen, the path will be complex for Frankie.

My regrets are sometimes serious in nature, at other times petty and sadly superficial. Will I be as affectionate with Frankie once he fully transitions? How will I feel as his voice changes? When he grows full facial hair? Will he continue to be more aggressive or aloof? Will he be more "boy-like" in his behaviour? Will he love me in the same way?

I feel wistful looking at friends' daughters' pictures on social media, dressed in their prom dresses with their dates, having princess parties for their birthdays, having girlie nights with their friends. I miss the dresses, the cute toys, and the little extra things one does for a little girl. Painting our nails. Talking about cute boys on TV. Watching Frankie experiment with new clothes, new shoes, jewellery. I miss combing Frankie's long, dark hair and buying her fun T-shirts and sneakers and little girlie things in the drugstore that I thought she might like. It's more complex than the baby lust that mothers experience as their children grow up — it's a nostalgia for the indulgence in the identity of having a little or young girl as a daughter.

As I write these words, the government papers have arrived officially changing Frankie's legal name to River. A new name, a new path. For him. For us.

And what of that unfinished dollhouse, the one that remains hidden in the closet of the middle bedroom on the second floor of our house, beneath the winter coats, old clothes, and the small suitcases? Untouched and unfinished. Will it be finished? Who will finish it? Will I complete it by myself? Or an older, calmer version of me, ten years from now, surrounded by one or two grandchildren — a little girl, or perhaps a little boy, or both?

But if I build it, I won't build it for them. I will build it for myself without the expectation that they will enjoy it. I won't press them to help me. I won't expect them to love it as much as I do. I will resolve to honour their wishes and desires, their dreams and aspirations. I promise I will let them be the people they were destined to be.

# A Post-Script About the Child Youth and Family Clinic at CAMH

✦

ON DECEMBER 15, 2015 IT was announced that the Gender Identity Clinic for children and youth at CAMH was officially winding down. According to a news source, an external review paid for by CAMH was conducted by Dr. Suzanne Zinck, Dalhousie University, and Dr. Antonio Pignatiello, Hospital for Sick Children. They found the approach of the clinic "was out of step with currently accepted practice." The clinic was accused of conducting "reparative, or conversion, therapy" — a charge that was denied by staff. CAMH has promised to create a three-prong plan to improve its services for transgender patients. While it will continue to provide services for its current clientele — roughly twenty to twenty-five young clients — it plans to consult the transgender community and academics in this field on future programs and services.

The Clinic has been very controversial within the trans community. I was personally made aware of this controversy by my own child just a few weeks after we became involved with the Clinic in 2013. By then, I was too uneasy with my own personal circumstances to try and seek assistance elsewhere. I had no idea where else to access services. Although I saw no evidence of reparative therapy and none was exerted upon River, my son remained sceptical of the Clinic at times. He felt that his progression towards transition was deliberately slowed down. River was told by staff that he was too gender-fluid for hormone therapy prior to the age of seventeen. This infuriated him.

However, in our involvement with the Clinic, I personally felt that we were treated with respect and processed in a timely fashion and I am grateful that they were able to assist us in a time of great distress and confusion. Whatever transpired, it is disturbing that there are now fewer organizations to assist children and youth in an area that is vastly underserviced by the medical establishment.

# A New Vocabulary

❖

*Agender:* A term that can be translated as "without gender".

*Androgynous:* The combination of masculine and feminine characteristics.

*AFab or DFab:* Assigned female at birth or designated female at birth.

*AMab or DMab:* Assigned male at birth or designated male at birth.

*Binding:* The process of flattening one's chest.

*Cis gender:* Describing a person who is not transgender/exclusively identifies with the gender they were assigned at birth.

*FTM:* Female to Male, a term used to describe a transgender male, designated/assigned female at birth.

*Gender Dysphoria:* The feeling of discomfort with a certain part of one's body that is associated with a gender other than theirs.

*Genderfluid:* Having a fluctuating gender identity.

*Gender Queer:* Denoting or relating to a person who does not subscribe to conventional gender distinctions but identifies with the binary genders male and female, neither, both or a combination of genders in and outside of the gender spectrum.

*Non-binary:* A catch-all category for gender identities which are not exclusively the binary genders male and female.

*Sexual Orientation:* A person's attraction to the gender(s) that they are attracted to; the fact of being heterosexual, homosexual, bisexual, pansexual, asexual, etc.

*Stealth:* The action(s) of a trans or gender noncomforming person not disclosing their gender identity, usually to promote privacy/safety.

*They, Their, and Them:* Gender neutral pronouns replacing S/he, Her/Him, Hers/His (also used Xe, Xem, Xyr).

*Transfeminine:* A gender identity used to describe those who were assigned male at birth (AMab) but identify as a gender closer to the feminine end of the gender spectrum.

*Transgender Man (Trans man):* A transgender person who was assigned female at birth but whose gender identity is that of a man.

*Transgender Woman (Trans woman):* A transgender person who was assigned male at birth but whose gender identity is that of a woman.

*Transitioning:* The process of changing one's gender presentation, to accord with one's sense of their own gender(s).

# Acknowledgements

This book is the culmination of many years of soul searching about how to describe the path that our son River has been on since he was twelve years of age and realized that the expectations placed on him felt wrong and had to be confronted and corrected. I would like to thank the following people:

Members of my writing group who assisted me in preparing this manuscript for submission — Arif Anwar, Michelle Boone, Justine Mazin, Josée Seguin, Liz Torlee, Tina Tzatzanis — who vanquished adverbs and superfluous clauses with dexterity and kindness. Their emotional support was invaluable during the writing of this memoir.

Mia famiglia — in particular my mother Antonia, brother Charlie, and sister Francesca and their families, including Belinda, Mara, Isabella, and Tony, as well my in-laws Tami & Terry, Todd & Julie, and their families — Kiya, Max, and Alex. Some cultural stereotypes are true. My family is ferociously loyal, loving, and possessed of enormous hearts.

My editor and publisher Marc Côté, who has exquisite

editing skills and a boundless generosity of spirit. I am grateful to Marc for expanding the central metaphor of the memoir. He is not only my editor but a much valued friend now.

My husband Rob, an unmatchable husband and father offered unconditional support, love and a calming influence through River's transition and in the writing of this memoir.

And most importantly, my son River, the bravest person I know and the inspiration for this memoir, who urged me to proceed in my writing when my energy was depleted and I felt I couldn't proceed. He represents the best part of my life. He helped me tear down the fantasy of the dollhouse I imposed on him ... brick by brick.

# About the Author

Michelle Alfano's fiction and non-fiction have been published in Canada and the United States. Her short story "Opera" was a finalist for the Journey Prize. Made up of Arias, the novella based on that story, won the 2010 F.G. Bressani Prize for short fiction. From 2013 to 2015, she was the associate Editor-in-Chief (Administraion) of the legendary literary quarterly *Descant*. *The Unfinished Dollhouse* is her first full-length work of narrative non-fiction.